PRAYER

BATTLE (2)

D1585676

DR D. K. OLUKOYA

General Overseer

Mountain Of Fire and Miracles Ministries Worldwide

2021 A .D. Seventy Days Fasting & Prayer Programme
English
(Dr D. K. Olukoya)

ISBN 978-978-920-234-8

© 2021 A .D.

A publication of:
MOUNTAIN OF FIRE AND MIRACLES MINISTRIES
13, Olasimbo Street, off Olumo Road,
(By UNILAG Second Gate), Onike, Iwaya
P. O. Box 2990, Sabo, Yaba, Lagos.
E-Mail: mfmhqworldwide@mountainoffire.org
Web-site: www.mountainoffire.org

I salute my wonderful wife, Pastor Shade, for her invaluable support in the ministry. I appreciate her unquantifiable support in the book ministry as the cover designer, art editor and art adviser.

All Scriptures are quoted from the King James version of the Bible

ISBN 978-978-920-234-8

9 789789 202348

PRAYER BATTLE (2)

Preface

"O Thou that hearest prayer, unto thee shall all flesh come" (Ps 65:2).

We give all the glory to the Lord for what He has been doing with our annual Seventy days prayer and fasting programme. The Lord has used the programme to: ignite the fire of revival in thousands of lives, put stubborn pursuers to flight, produce prayer eagles, open chapters of prosperity for many, confuse satanic dribblers and put the enemies' gear in reverse. Prayer is of great value in turbulent and non-turbulent situations. Prayer is a necessity not an option.

"Howbeit this kind goeth not out but by PRAYER AND FASTING" (Matt 17:21).

Some mountains will not fall unless they are bombarded with the artillery of prayer and fasting.

The weapon of prayer and fasting have been known to do wonders when other methods have failed. In addition, some breakthroughs are impossible unless there is regular, consistent, concerted, constant bombardment of prayers. The prayer points for this year's programme have been specially vomited by the Holy Ghost to bring salvation, deliverance and healing of the spirit, soul and body to God's people. Pray them with determination, pray them with aggression, pray them with violence in your spirit, pray them with violent faith, pray them with great expectation and your life will never remain the same. The God who answereth by fire will surely answer you, in Jesus' name.

Your friend in the school of prayer,

Dr D. K. OLUKOYA

DEVOTIONAL HYMNS

Lord, Her Watch Thy Church is Keeping

Everton 87 87 D

Henry Smart

HYMN NUMBER 1 LORD, HER WATCH THY CHURCH IS KEEPING

1. *p* Lord, her watch Thy Church is keeping
When shall earth Thy rule obey?
When shall end the night of weeping?
When shall break the promised day?
   cr See the whitening harvest languish,
Waiting still the laborers' toil;
   mf Was it vain, Thy Son's deep anguish?
Shall the Strong retain the spoil?

2. *f* Tidings, sent to every creature,
Millions yet have never heard:
Can they hear without a preacher?
Lord Almighty, give the word!

cr Give the word! In every nation
Let the gospel trumpet sound,
f Witnessing a world's salvation,
To the earth's remotest bound

3. *f* Then the end! Thy Church completed,
All Thy chosen gathered in,
With their King in glory seated,
Satan bound, and banished sin;
mp Gone for ever parting, weeping,
Hunger, sorrow, death, and pain;
Lo! Her watch Thy Church is keeping;
cr Come, Lord Jesus, come to reign!

It Is A Thing Most Wonderful

Thomas Bishop Southgate

HYMN NUMBER 2 - IT IS A THING MOST WONDERFUL

1. *mf* It is a thing most wonderful,
Almost too wonderful to be,
mp That God's own Son should come from heaven,
And die to save a child like me.

2. *p* And yet I know that it is true:
He chose a poor and humble lot,
pp And wept and toiled and mourned and died
For love of those who loved him not.

3. *mp* I cannot tell how he could love
A child so weak and full of sin;
cr His love must be most wonderful,
mf If he could die my love to win.

4. *f* It is most wonderful to know
His love for me so free and sure;
cr But 'tis more wonderful to see
mp My love for him so faint and poor.

5. *mp* And yet I want to love thee, Lord;
cr O light the flame within my heart,
f And I will love thee more and more,
Until I see thee as thou art.

Lord, Enthroned in Heavenly Splendour

George Hugh B.

George C. Martins

HYMN NUMBER 3 - LORD, ENTHRONED IN HEAV'NLY SPLENDOR

1. *f* Lord, enthroned in heav'nly splendor,
First-begotten from the dead,
mf Thou alone, our strong Defender,
cr Liftest up Thy people's head.
f Alleluia! Alleluia!
Jesus, true and living Bread!

2. *mp* Here our humblest homage pay we,
Here in loving rev'rence bow:
Here for faith's discernment pray we,
Lest we fail to know thee now.
f Alleluia! Alleluia!
Thou art here, we ask not how.

3. *p* Though the lowliest form doth veil thee
As of old in Bethlehem,
cr Here as there thine angels hail thee,

Branch and Flow'r of Jesse's Stem.
f Alleluia! Alleluia!
We in worship join with them

4. *mf* Paschal Lamb! Thine off'ring finished
Once for all when Thou wast slain
In its fullness undiminished
Shall for evermore remain.
f Alleluia! Alleluia!
Cleansing souls from ev'ry stain.

5. *mf* Life-imparting heav'nly Manna,
Stricken Rock, with streaming side,
cr Heav'n and earth with loud hosanna
Worship Thee, the Lamb who died.
f Alleluia! Alleluia!
Ris'n, ascended, glorified!

I've Been Changed

Mosie Lister

HYMN NUMBER 4 - WELL, I'VE BEEN TO THE RIVER, I'VE BEEN BAPTIZED

1. *mf* Well, I've been to the river, I've been baptized;
I've been washed in the blood of the lamb,
I've been changed from the creature that once I was,
And redeemed is now my name.

Chorus
  f I've been changed
    I'm a new born now
All my life has been rearranged
What a difference it made,
When the Lord came and stayed,
In my heart, oh yes, I've been changed.

2. *mp* Though my sins were as scarlet, they're white as snow,

I was bound but today, I am free,
I was lost in the darkness but now am found,
I was blind but now I see.

3. *mp* Like the poor Hebrew children, I wandered long,
In a bare desert land to and fro;
  f But I crossed over Jordan to Canaan's land,
Where the milk and honey flow.

4. *f* When at last in His presence I stand above,
He will wipe all the tears from my eyes;
And I'll thank Him for giving a wretch like me,
Lasting hope beyond the skies.

The Resurrection Mourn

Dutch Melody (17th cent.)

VRUECHTEN 67.67.D.

HYMN NUMBER 5 - THE RESURRECTION MORN

1. *f*   The resurrection morn,
      Away with care and sorrow!
mp My Love, the Crucified,
cr   Hath sprung to life that morning.

Refrain
mp Had Christ, that once was slain,
      Ne'er burst His three day prison,
p   Our faith had been in vain;
cr   But now hath Christ arisen,
cr   Arisen, arisen, arisen!

2. *mp* My flesh in hope shall rest,
       And for a season slumber;
cr   Till trump from east to west,
f   Shall wake the dead in number.

3. *f*   Death's flood hath lost his chill,
      Since Jesus crossed the river:
mp Lover of souls, from ill
       My passing soul deliver.

PRAYER BATTLE (2)

OH JESUS I HAVE PROMISED

AURELIA   Samuel Sabastian Wesley (1864)

HYMN NUMBER 6 - O JESUS, I HAVE PROMISED

1. *mp* O Jesus, I have promised
To serve Thee to the end;
Be Thou forever near me,
My Master and my Friend:
I shall not fear the battle
If Thou art by my side,
Nor wander from the pathway
If Thou wilt be my guide.

2. O let me feel Thee near me,
The world is ever near;
I see the sights that dazzle,
The tempting sounds I hear:

di My foes are ever near me,
Around me and within;

cr But, Jesus, draw Thou nearer,
And shield my soul from sin.

3. *p* O let me hear Thee speaking
In accents clear and still,
Above the storms of passion,
The murmurs of selfwill,

cr O speak to reassure me,
To hasten or control;
O speak, and make me listen,
Thou Guardian of my soul.

PRAYER BATTLE (2)

4. *mf* O Jesus, Thou hast promised
        To all who follow Thee,
        That where Thou art in glory,
        There shall Thy servant be;
        And, Jesus, I have promised
        To serve Thee to the end;
        O give me grace to follow,
        My Master and my Friend.

5. *p* O let me see Thy footmarks
        And in them plant mine own;
        My hope to follow duly
        Is in Thy strength alone,
        O guide me, call me, draw me,
        Uphold me to the end;
        And then in heaven receive me,
        My Saviour and my Friend.

Hymn for the Vigil

HYMN FOR THE VIGIL

HEAR THE FOOTSTEPS OF JESUS(13.13.12.12 & Ref)

For I am the Lord that healeth thee (Exod. 15:26)

W.J.K   W.J.KIRKPATRICK

1.*f* Hear the footsteps of Jesus,
      He is now passing by,
      Bearing balm for the wounded,
      Healing all who apply;
      As He spake to the suff'rer

Who lay at the pool,
He is saying this moment,
"Wilt thou be made whole?"
Refrain
mf Wilt thou be made whole?

PRAYER BATTLE (2)

Wilt thou be made whole?

P   Oh come, weary suff'rer,
Oh come, sin-sick soul;

ƒ   See the life-stream is flowing,
See the cleansing waves roll,
Step into the current and thou shalt be
whole.

2.ƒ   'Tis the voice of that Savior,
Whose merciful call
Freely offers salvation
To one and to all;
He is now beck'ning to Him
Each sin-tainted soul,
And lovingly asking,
"Wilt thou be made whole?"

3. *mf* Are you halting and struggling,
Overpowr'd by your sin,
While the waters are troubled
Can you not enter in?

ƒ   Lo, the Savior stands waiting
To strengthen your soul;
He is earnestly pleading,
"Wilt thou be made whole?"

4. *mp* Blessed Savior, assist us
To rest on Thy Word;
Let the soul healing power
On us now be outpoured;
Wash away every sin-spot,
Take perfect control,
Say to each trusting spirit,
"Thy faith makes thee whole."

PRAYER BATTLE (2)

TO BE SAID DAILY

Father, in the name of Jesus, I thank You for:

1. Drawing me to prayer and power,
2. The salvation of my soul,
3. Baptizing me with the Holy Spirit,
4. Producing spiritual gifts upon my life,
5. The fruit of the Spirit working in me,
6. The wonderful gift of praise,
7. All the ways You have intervened in my affairs,
8. Your divine plan for my life,
9. You will never leave me nor forsake me,
10. Bringing me to a place of maturity and deeper life,
11. Lifting me up when I fall,
12. Keeping me in perfect peace,
13. Making all things work together for good for me,
14. Protecting me from the snares of the fowler and from the noisome pestilence,
15. The wonder-working power in Your Word and in the Blood of the Lamb,
16. Giving Your angels charge over me,
17. Fighting for me against my adversaries,
18. Making me more than a conqueror,
19. Supplying all my needs according to Your riches in glory,
20. Your healing power upon my body, soul and spirit,
21. Flooding my heart with the light of heaven,
22. Always causing me to triumph in Christ Jesus,
23. Turning my curses into blessings,
24. Enabling me to dwell in safety,
25. All the blessings of life,
26. Your greatness, power, glory, majesty, splendor and righteousness,
27. Silencing the foe and the avenger,

PRAYER BATTLE (2)

28. You are at my right hand and I shall not be moved,

29. You are trustworthy and will help Your own,

30. Not allowing my enemies to rejoice over me,

31. Your wonderful love,

32. You are great and greatly to be praised,

33. Delivering my soul from death and my feet from stumbling,

34. You are my fortress and refuge in time of trouble,

35. Your faithfulness and marvellous deeds,

36. Your act of power and surpassing greatness,

37. Dispersing spiritual blindness from my spirit,

38. Lifting me out of the depths,

39. Preserving me and keeping my feet from slipping,

40. Your name is a strong tower, the righteous runs into it and he is safe.

PRAYERS FOR CHURCH, MISSIONARY ACTIVITIES AND CHRISTIAN HOMES

TO BE SAID EVERY SUNDAY

1. Thank You, Father, for the promise which says, "I will build my church and the gates of hell shall not prevail against it."

2. I ask for forgiveness of every sin causing disunity and powerlessness in the body of Christ.

3. I take authority over the power of darkness in all its ramifications, in Jesus' name.

4. I bind and cast out every spirit causing seduction, false doctrine, deception, hypocrisy, pride and error, in Jesus' name.

5. Every plan and strategy of satan against the body of Christ, be bound, in the name of Jesus.

6. Every spirit of prayerlessness, discouragement and vainglory in the body of Christ, be bound, in the name of Jesus.

7. Father, let the spirit of brokenness be released upon us, in Jesus' name.

8. I command the works of the flesh in the lives of the brethren to die, in Jesus' name.

9. Let the power of the cross and of the Holy Spirit be released to dethrone flesh in our lives, in the name of Jesus.

10. Let the life of our Lord Jesus Christ be truly established in the body of Christ, in the name of Jesus.

11. Every power of selfishness, over-ambition and unteachableness, be broken, in the name of Jesus.

12. Father, grant unto the body of Christ the mind of Christ, forgiving spirit, tolerance, genuine repentance, understanding, submission, humility, brokenness, watchfulness and the mind to commend others better than ourselves, in Jesus' name.

13. I challenge and pull down the forces of disobedience in the lives of the saints, in the name of Jesus.

PRAYER BATTLE (2)

14. I command these blessings on the body of Christ and ministers

- love   - joy   - peace   - longsuffering
- gentleness   - goodness   - faith   - meekness
- temperance   - divine healing   - divine health   - fruitfulness
- progress   - faith   - the gifts of healing
- prophecy   - discerning of spirits   - the word of wisdom
- the word of knowledge   - the working of miracles
- divers kinds of tongues   - the interpretation of tongues
- beauty and glory of God   - righteousness and holiness
- dedication and commitment

15. Father, create the thirst and hunger for God and holiness in our lives, in the name of Jesus.

16. O Lord, send down the fire of revival into the body of Christ.

17. O Lord, break and refill Your ministers and vessels afresh.

18. Let there be a full and fresh outpouring of the Holy Ghost upon the ministers of God, in the name of Jesus.

19. O Lord, give unto Your ministers the power for effective prayer life.

20. O Lord, release faithful, committed, dedicated and obedient labourers into the vineyard.

21. I break down the authority and dominion of satan over the souls of men, in the name of Jesus.

22. Every spirit holding the souls of men in captivity, I shatter your backbone, in the name of Jesus.

23. Every covenant between the souls of men and satan, I dash you to pieces, in the name of Jesus.

24. Let the spirit of steadfastness, consistency, hunger and thirst for the word of God come upon the converts, in Jesus' name.

25. O Lord, release fresh fire to disgrace territorial spirits upon all our missionaries and evangelists, in the name of Jesus.

26. I break the power and the grip of the world upon the souls of men, in Jesus'

name.

27. I release the spirit of salvation upon areas that have not been reached by the gospel, in the name of Jesus.

28. O Lord, remove all the hindrances to Your purpose for Christian homes.

29. I command the spirits of quarrel, immorality, unfaithfulness, infirmity, disagreement, misunderstanding and intolerance to lose their grips upon Christian homes, in the name of Jesus.

30. Let all Christian homes be a light to the world and a vehicle of salvation, in the name of Jesus.

31. O God, raise up Esther, Ruth and Deborah in this generation, in Jesus' name.

32. Every power destroying joy in the home, be dismantled, in Jesus' name.

33. O Lord, grant us special wisdom to train our children in Your glory.

34. Every Christian marriage that has been re-arranged by the enemy, be corrected, in the name of Jesus.

35. O Lord, let the spirits of wisdom, judgement, submission, gentleness, obedience to God's word and faithfulness in the home, come upon Christian homes, in the name of Jesus.

36. O Lord, remove every wrong spirit from the midst of Your children and put in the right spirit, in the name of Jesus.

37. I take authority over the plans and activities of satan on ministers' homes, in the name of Jesus.

38. O Lord, increase the power and strength of the ministration of Your word amongst us, in the name of Jesus.

39. Father, let the kingdom of Christ come into every nation by fire, in Jesus' name.

40. O Lord, dismantle every man-made programme in the body of Christ and set up Your own programme.

PRAYERS FOR THE NATION

TO BE SAID ON FRIDAYS

SCRIPTURES: 1Tim 2:1-2: **I exhort therefore, that, first of all, supplications, prayers, intercessions, and giving of thanks, be made for all men; For kings, and for all that are in authority; that we may lead a quiet and peaceable life in all godliness and honesty.**

Jer 1:10: **See, I have this day set thee over the nations and over the kingdoms, to root out, and to pull down, and to destroy, and to throw down, to build, and to plant.**

Other Scriptures: Isa 61:1-6; Eph 6:10-16.

Praise Worship

1. Father, in the name of Jesus, I confess all the sins and iniquities of the land, of our ancestors, of our leaders, and of the people. E.g., violence, rejection of God, corruption, idolatry, robbery, suspicion, injustice, bitterness, bloody riots, pogroms, rebellion, conspiracy, shedding of innocent blood, tribal conflicts, child-kidnapping and murder, occultism, mismanagement, negligence, etc.

2. I plead for mercy and forgiveness, in the name of Jesus.

3. O Lord, remember our land and redeem it.

4. O Lord, save our land from destruction and judgement.

5. O Lord, let Your healing power begin to operate upon our land, in Jesus' name.

6. All forces of darkness hindering the move of God in this nation, be rendered impotent, in the name of Jesus.

7. I command the spiritual strong man in charge of this country to be bound and be disgraced, in the name of Jesus.

8. Every evil establishment and satanic tree in this country, be uprooted and cast into fire, in the name of Jesus.

9. I come against every spirit of the anti-Christ working against this nation and I command it to be permanently frustrated, in the name of Jesus.

10. I command the stones of fire from God to fall upon every national satanic operation and activity, in Jesus' name.

11. O Lord, let the desires, plans, devices and expectations of the enemy for this

country be completely frustrated, in Jesus' name.

12. Every satanic curse on this nation, fall down to the ground and die, in Jesus' name.

13. By the blood of Jesus, let all sins, ungodliness, idolatry and vices cease in the land, in the name of Jesus.

14. I break every evil covenant and dedication made upon our land, in Jesus' name.

15. I plead the blood of Jesus over the nation, in Jesus' name.

16. I decree the will of God for this land, whether the devil likes it or not, in the name of Jesus.

17. All contrary powers and authorities in Nigeria, be confounded and be put to shame, in the name of Jesus.

18. I close every satanic gate in every city of this country, in Jesus' name.

19. Every evil throne in this country, be dashed to pieces, in Jesus' name.

20. I bind all negative forces operating in the lives of the leaders of this country, in the name of Jesus.

21. O Lord, lay Your hands of fire and power upon all our leaders, in the name of Jesus.

22. I bind every blood-drinking demon in this country, in Jesus' name.

23. O Lord, let the Prince of Peace reign in every department of this nation, in the name of Jesus.

24. Every anti-gospel spirit, be frustrated and be rendered impotent, in Jesus' name.

25. O Lord, give us leaders who will see their roles as a calling, instead of an opportunity to amass wealth.

26. All forms of ungodliness, be destroyed by the divine fire of burning, in Jesus' name.

27. O Lord, let our leaders be filled with divine understanding and wisdom, in the name of Jesus.

28. O Lord, let our leaders follow the counsel of God and not of man and demons, in the name of Jesus.

29. O Lord, let our leaders have wisdom and knowledge of God, in Jesus' name.

30. O Lord, let our government be the kind that would obtain Your direction and leading, in the name of Jesus.

31. Every satanic altar, in this country, receive the fire of God and burn to ashes, in the name of Jesus.

32. I silence every satanic prophet, priest and practitioner, in the mighty name of Jesus. I forbid them from interfering with the affairs of this nation, in the name of Jesus.

33. Blood of Jesus, cleanse our land from every blood pollution, in the name of Jesus.

34. I command the fire of God on all idols, sacrifices, rituals, shrines and local satanic thrones in this country, in Jesus' name.

35. I break any conscious and unconscious agreement made between the people of this country and satan, in Jesus' name.

36. I dedicate and claim all our cities for Jesus, in Jesus' name.

37. Father, let the blessings and presence of the Lord be experienced in all our cities, in the name of Jesus.

38. I decree total paralysis on lawlessness, immorality and drug addiction in this country, in the name of Jesus.

39. Father, let the power, love and glory of God be established in our land, in the name of Jesus.

40. O Lord, let there be thirst and hunger for God in the hearts of Christians of this nation, in the name of Jesus.

41. O Lord, deposit the spirit of revival in Nigeria.

42. O Lord, lay Your hands of power and might upon the Armed Forces and the Police, all government establishments and institutions, all universities and colleges in this country, in the name of Jesus.

43. O Lord, let the resurrection power of the Lord Jesus Christ fall upon our economy, in the name of Jesus.

44. Father, let there be fruitfulness and prosperity in every area of this country, in the name of Jesus.

45. I command every threat to the political, economic and social stability in the

land to be paralysed, in the name of Jesus.

46. I frustrate every satanic external influence over our nation, in Jesus' name.

47. I command confusion and disagreement among the sons of the bond woman planning to cage the nation, in Jesus' name.

48. I break any covenant between any satanic external influence and our leaders, in the name of Jesus.

49. I paralyse every spirit of wastage of economic resources in this country, in the name of Jesus.

50. Spirit of borrowing, depart completely from this country, in the name of Jesus.

51. O Lord, show Yourself mighty in the affairs of this nation.

52. Father, let the Kingdom of Christ come into this nation, in Jesus' name.

53. O Lord, do new things in our country to show Your power and greatness to the heathens, in the name of Jesus.

54. Father, let the Kingdom of our Lord Jesus Christ come into the heart of every person in this country, in the name of Jesus.

55. O Lord, have mercy upon this nation, in the name of Jesus.

56. All the glory of this nation, that has departed, be restored, in Jesus' name.

57. Father, let all un-evangelised areas of this country, be reached with the gospel of our Lord Jesus Christ, in the name of Jesus.

58. O Lord, send forth labourers into Your vineyard to reach the unreached in this country, in the name of Jesus.

59. I dismantle the stronghold of poverty in this nation, in the name of Jesus.

60. O Lord, install Your agenda for this nation.

61. Every power of darkness, operating in our educational institutions, be disgraced, in the name of Jesus.

62. Satanic representatives of key posts in this country, be dismantled, in Jesus' name.

63. Every evil spiritual throne behind all physical thrones in Nigeria, be dismantled, in the name of Jesus.

64. Every satanic covenant, made on behalf of this country, by anyone, be nullified, in the name of Jesus.

PRAYER BATTLE (2)

65. I trample upon the serpents and scorpions of ethnic clashes in this country, in the name of Jesus.

66. I decree a realignment of the situation around Christians, to favour them in this country, in the name of Jesus.

67. I dethrone every strange king installed in the spirit realm over this country, in the name of Jesus.

68. All principalities, powers, rulers of darkness and spiritual wickedness in heavenly places, militating against this nation, be bound and be disgraced, in the name of Jesus.

69. Lord, let righteousness reign in every part of this nation, in Jesus' name.

70. Praises.

SECTION 1 - WIPING OFF DARK HANDWRITING

Scripture Reading: Matthew 27
Confession: Colossians 2:14-15: Blotting out the handwriting of ordinances that was against us, which was contrary to us, and took it out of the way, nailing it to his cross; And having spoiled principalities and powers, he made a shew of them openly, triumphing over them in it.

Day 1 *(09-08-21) The Bible in 70 Days (Day 1 - Gen 1:1- 18:20)*
Devotional Songs (Pages 4-10)
Praise and Worship
Prayers of Praise and Thanksgiving (Page 13)

1. Powers saying it is a waste of time for me to pray, receive angelic slap, in the name of Jesus.

2. The battle that has not started in my life but is coming, O God, arise and swallow it, in the name of Jesus.

3. The battle that has started in my life, which I have not known, O God, swallow it, in the name of Jesus.

4. O God, arise and bring me out of the room that does not favour my destiny, in the name of Jesus.

5. Powers negotiating a revenge against me, be wasted, in the name of Jesus.

6. Evil anointed words fighting against me, backfire, in the name of Jesus.

7. Every darkness that has covered the face of my life, catch fire, in Jesus' name.

8. Anyone dragging my destiny ladder with me, run mad and die, in Jesus' name.

9. Powers biting me in secret, thunder of God, expose them and strike them to death, in the name of Jesus.

10. O God, arise and snatch the joy of the evil man expecting evil to manifest in my life, in the name of Jesus.

11. Whenever my enemy calls my name, my destiny will not answer, in the name of Jesus.

12. Dangerous source of wicked powers against me, catch fire, in Jesus' name.

13. Dark powers using my destiny to prepare charms, receive the arrow of destruction, in the name of Jesus.

14. Magic powers threatening my life, catch fire, in the name of Jesus.

PRAYER BATTLE (2)

15. Wicked elders sharing my glory to strangers, die, in the name of Jesus.

16. Wicked powers giving me sleepless nights, leave my life alone and die, in the name of Jesus.

17. Thunder of God, arise and waste my enemies at their unguarded hours, in the name of Jesus.

18. I blow the ashes of fire into the eyes of my enemies, in the name of Jesus.

19. Demonic powers that are calling my name from the evil forest, shut up and die, in the name of Jesus.

20. O God, let Your fire consume every waster of my destiny to death, in the name of Jesus.

21. Powers that are on assignment to make me cry, so that they can say to me 'sorry', be disappointed, in the name of Jesus.

22. O Lord, hit the head of my enemies for their memories of me to die, in the name of Jesus.

23. Powers that see glory and kill it, leave my life alone and die, in Jesus' name.

24. Anyone keeping vigil to see me shattered, run mad and die, in Jesus' name.

25. Any power putting my name on the list of sudden death, die in my place, in the name of Jesus.

26. Wicked herbalist seeking my destiny to solve other people's problems, run mad and die, in the name of Jesus.

27. Powers making it difficult for me to lift up my head, O God, arise, use their heads as sacrifices for my rising, in the name of Jesus.

28. My mouth shall not become my grave, in the name of Jesus.

Day 2 (10-08-21) *The Bible in 70 Days (Day 2 - Gen 18:21 - 31:16)*
Devotional Songs (Pages 4-10)
Praise and Worship
Prayers of Praise and Thanksgiving (Page 13)

29. Arrow of sorrow and weeping, fired into my life, backfire, in the name of Jesus.

30. Powers rearranging my destiny to be an emptier, be disappointed, in the name of Jesus.

31. Every arrow chasing me away from my place of blessings, backfire, in the name

of Jesus.

32. Powers using my shadow to send me arrows, use your hands against yourselves, in the name of Jesus.

33. Powers sending demons to use my shadow to scare me to death, be wasted by fire, in the name of Jesus.

34. Powers pushing me into the business that will waste my life, fail woefully, in the name of Jesus.

35. My name, written before evil shrine, become terror, in the name of Jesus.

36. Powers pursuing my blood for fun, be wasted in your own blood, in the name of Jesus.

37. Powers burying my virtues in any satanic coffin, catch fire, in Jesus' name.

38. Cemetery demons claiming me as their friend, I reject you by fire, in the name of Jesus.

39. O God, arise and break the chain dragging me into the coffin of darkness, in the name of Jesus.

40. Voice of darkness commanding me into a coffin, be silent by fire, in the name of Jesus.

41. Poverty attached to my glory, die, in the name of Jesus.

42. Net of my destiny, hear the voice of the Lord, break no more, in Jesus' name.

43. Powers waiting to break my net, I will see you no more, in the name of Jesus.

44. Evil manifestation in whatever I touch, expire, in the name of Jesus.

45. Anyone born of a woman, presently using my glory, your time is up, release it, in the name of Jesus.

46. Powers attacking what I will become in life, receive the arrow of death, in the name of Jesus.

47. Who is that person using my glory to take stars in the evil society? Die and scatter by the thunder of God, in the name of Jesus

48. Every evil bird dragging my destiny away, catch fire, in the name of Jesus.

49. My day of success, blocked by witchcraft bird, be unblocked by fire, in the name of Jesus.

50. Antagonistic birds at the point of my success and my breakthroughs, receive

the judgement of God and die, in the name of Jesus.

51. I command the witchcraft bird, flying across my room whenever good things are about to locate me, to catch fire and die, in the name of Jesus.

52. O God, arise and trouble those using evil birds to trouble my destiny, in the name of Jesus.

53. Powers boasting against my life, anger of God, destroy them, in Jesus' name.

54. O God, arise and fight for my glory and my destiny, in the name of Jesus.

55. Anyone that turned himself to a wasting power against me, waste yourself, in the name of Jesus.

56. Strange battles sent to catch up with me, backfire, in the name of Jesus.

Day 3 (11-08-21) - *The Bible in 70 Days (Day 3 - Genesis 31:17 - 44:10)*
Devotional Songs (Pages 4-10)
Praise and Worship
Prayers of Praise and Thanksgiving (Page 13)

57. Battle against permanent solution to my problem, scatter by fire, in the name of Jesus

58. O God, arise and end the strange curses in my life, in the name of Jesus.

59. O God, arise and make my problem a forgotten one, in the name of Jesus.

60. O God, arise and clear away all my battles, in the name of Jesus.

61. Powers saying: 'How will my battle be conquered?', O God, arise and disappoint them, in the name of Jesus.

62. Powers caging my helpers, catch fire, in the name of Jesus.

63. You, the fire of my glory, you must not quench, in the name of Jesus.

64. Wicked ones, assigned to kill the fire of my glory, dry up, in the name of Jesus.

65. Powers waiting to say 'it is finished for me', die a shameful death, in the name of Jesus.

66. Powers behind my case and mocking me over my situation, receive the arrow of death, in the name of Jesus.

67. Battles making everyone that sees me to hate me, scatter by fire, in the name of Jesus.

68. O Lord, let me not be my own enemy when my blessings come, in Jesus' name.

69. Powers assigned to cage me in a helpless situation, O God, arise and judge them quickly, in the name of Jesus.

70. O God, arise and release Your anger against my oppressors, in Jesus' name.

71. Powers hiding to destroy me, O God, arise and release Your anger against them, in the name of Jesus.

72. Demonic cane sent to flog me, backfire, in the name of Jesus.

73. What the enemy knows about me, that he is using to make me suffer, expire by fire, in the name of Jesus.

74. Every battle suddenly confronting me, be terminated now, in Jesus' name.

75. Powers assigned to make me wine and dine with disgrace, die, in Jesus' name.

76. The secrets the enemy knows that I do not know and that will make me great; O God, arise, let my enemy forget them and let them be revealed to me, in the name of Jesus.

77. Powers that want to use my secret to imprison my destiny, O God, beat them to death, in the name of Jesus.

78. Powers in their wicked hiding place, sending arrows to me, fire of God, consume them, in the name of Jesus.

79. Whoever is at the point of destroying me, fire of God, consume him, in the name of Jesus.

80. Evildoers that are restless because of me, let all your wicked efforts revert to you, in the name of Jesus.

81. Anyone in the room of darkness because of me, O God, arise and use death to clear him away, in the name of Jesus.

82. Where my enemies say I will never be the head, O Lord, make me the head, in the name of Jesus.

83. O God, arise and destroy the evil eyes focussed on me, in the name of Jesus.

84. Evil eyes closing the door of my deliverance, catch fire, in the name of Jesus.

Day 4 (12-08-21) - *The Bible in 70 Days (Day 4 - Gen 44:11 - Exod 1:1-10:2)*

Devotional Songs (Pages 4-10)
Praise and Worship
Prayers of Praise and Thanksgiving (Page 13)

85. Eyes of the elders drying up the well of my glory, catch fire, in Jesus' name.

86. Witchcraft crabs, working against my blessings, catch fire, in Jesus' name.

87. Powers using my destiny for an evil purpose, die, in the name of Jesus.

88. Any man stealing my destiny with money, run mad and die, in Jesus' name.

89. Evildoers stealing my destiny for evil powers, receive the arrow of death, in the name of Jesus.

90. Powers sitting on my destiny to have long life, die suddenly, in Jesus' name.

91. Powers pursuing my destiny for fame, be disgraced, in the name of Jesus.

92. Anyone caging me for good fortunes, leave my life alone and die, in the name of Jesus.

93. Anyone using charms to steal from me, run mad and die, in the name of Jesus.

94. Any evil ring that has touched my body to steal from me, catch fire, in the name of Jesus.

95. Every unwanted stranger in my destiny, die, in the name of Jesus.

96. Evil flow from my family, blocking my way, dry up, in the name of Jesus.

97. Every aroma of shame and disgrace in my life, expire, in the name of Jesus.

98. Favour arrester, leave my life alone and die, in the name of Jesus.

99. Glory of God, give me a new identity, in the name of Jesus.

100. Wicked powers sprinkling the water of poverty on my body, receive the arrow of death, in the name of Jesus.

101. Any broken window inviting the weapon of my enemies against me, be closed, in the name of Jesus.

102. Satanic birds sent to form a meeting point by my window, scatter by fire, in the name of Jesus.

103. Satanic birds sent to watch me, catch fire, in the name of Jesus.

104. Any power that needs to die or run mad, for me to dance and rejoice, die, in the name of Jesus.

PRAYER BATTLE (2)

105. I stand against any evil dream, in the name of Jesus.

106. Every problem that wants to turn me to a fool before my enemies, scatter by fire, in the name of Jesus.

107. Every strange bird assigned to mess up my day of celebration, catch fire, in the name of Jesus.

108. O God, arise and let there be a quick release for my open door, in the name of Jesus.

109. Every demonic animal assigned to report me to the kingdom of darkness, receive the arrow of death, in the name of Jesus.

110. Negative appearance of any evil bird in my life, catch fire, in Jesus' name.

111. Any evil bird sent to fly over my head to take my destiny crown, I recover my crown, die, in the name of Jesus.

112. Anything the enemies have taken from me through evil birds, be returned by fire, by force, in the name of Jesus.

Day 5 (13-08-21) - *The Bible in 70 Days (Day 5 - Exodus 10:3 - 25:29)*
Devotional Songs (Pages 4-10)
Praise and Worship
Prayers of Praise and Thanksgiving (Page 13)

113. Every sick bird assigned to bring sickness into my house, backfire, in the name of Jesus.

114. Evil birds perching on my glory, somersault and scatter, in Jesus' name.

115. Any evil message left in my house by dark powers, scatter by fire, in the name of Jesus.

116. Snail from the marine world, crawling around my body, catch fire, in the name of Jesus.

117. Mysterious dreams of backwardness, lose your hold, in the name of Jesus.

118. Every power that wants me to be too comfortable with the present state of my life, die, in the name of Jesus.

119. Powers advertising my village in my dream, die by fire, in the name of Jesus.

120. Any wicked power that wants me to leave the city and settle down in the village for demonic pity and mocking, be disappointed, in the name of Jesus.

PRAYER BATTLE (2)

121. Every wicked power using my placenta to summon me to evil places in the dream, receive the arrow of God and die, in the name of Jesus.

122. Every evil cloth of backwardness and suffering, put upon me by a particular person in my village, I return your evil garment to you, in the name of Jesus.

123. My head shall not be buried in the village, in the name of Jesus.

124. Any member of my family in the village, that wants me to be like him or act like him, I reject your expectation for me by fire, in the name of Jesus.

125. O God, arise and release fresh glory upon my life, in the name of Jesus.

126. My hidden virtues, hiding in the body of my enemy, come out and locate me, in the name of Jesus.

127. Evil mouth thirsty for my blood, catch fire, in the name of Jesus.

128. Darkness from the kingdom of darkness, assigned to kill me, clear away, in the name of Jesus.

129. Rage of the elders against my life, scatter, in the name of Jesus.

130. Wind of God, blow my enemies away, in the name of Jesus.

131. Powers hired to kill my helpers, die, in the name of Jesus.

132. Holy Ghost, push the enemies of my helpers away from them, in the name of Jesus.

133. I will not go before my enemies to beg for food, in the name of Jesus.

134. I hand over my troublers to the judgement of God, in the name of Jesus.

135. Powers that want me to be in the grave before my glory shines, be disappointed, in the name of Jesus.

136. Powers that want to put off the light of my virtues, lose your power and die, in the name of Jesus.

137. O God, arise and tear the house of my enemies down, in the name of Jesus.

138. Comfort of the enemies over my life, become their coffin, in Jesus' name.

139. Powers that want me to live in disgrace, be disappointed, in Jesus' name.

140. Terror of death pursuing my life, die, in the name of Jesus.

Day 6 (14-08-21) - *The Bible in 70 Days (Day 6 - Exodus 25:30 - 39:5)*

Devotional Songs (Pages 4-10)
Praise and Worship
Prayers of Praise and Thanksgiving (Page 13)

141. Destiny killer squads that are after my destiny, destroy yourselves, in the name of Jesus.

142. Battles assigned to turn me to a living dead, scatter by fire, in Jesus' name.

143. My unending laughter, appear and cease no more, in the name of Jesus.

144. Divine garment that covers nakedness, cover my nakedness, in Jesus' name.

145. My voice shall not be strange to heaven, in the name of Jesus.

146. Anger of God, scatter my enemies, in the name of Jesus.

147. Powers assigned to subject me to pain, die, in the name of Jesus.

148. O Lord, deliver my glory from the sins of my father and mother, in the name of Jesus.

149. My days of affliction, satanically set apart on evil calendars, be deleted by fire, in the name of Jesus.

150. O God, arise and destroy all evil men threatening my existence, in the name of Jesus.

151. Any hand behind my affliction, catch fire, in the name of Jesus.

152. Instant judgement of God, fall upon my strong enemies, in Jesus' name.

153. Any pot boiling my picture, break and scatter, in the name of Jesus.

154. The wicked ones behind the evil upsetting my life, O God, beat them to death, in the name of Jesus.

155. Powers that cannot rest until they bring me down, thunder of God, swallow them, in the name of Jesus.

156. O God, arise in Your fire and deliver me from the wicked fowls of the air, in the name of Jesus.

157. Battles sending me away from meeting the right people, be terminated now, in the name of Jesus.

158. Powers attracting people that will bring trouble into my life to me, be wasted, in the name of Jesus.

159. Powers saying it is a waste of time for me to pray, receive angelic slap, in the name of Jesus.

160. The battle that has not started in my life, satanically designed to occur, O God, arise and swallow it, in the name of Jesus.

161. The battle that has started in my life, but has not yet started to manifest, O God, swallow it, in the name of Jesus.

162. Battles from my home, hear the word of God, stay away from me, in the name of Jesus.

163. Battles from my place of work, hear the word of the Lord, stay away from me, in the name of Jesus.

164. Power of the Lord Jesus Christ, arise and let my battle be swallowed by the earth, in the name of Jesus.

165. O God, arise and let the sign of my destiny speak, in the name of Jesus.

166. O God, arise and let the sign You created with me appear, in Jesus' name.

167. Whoever is preparing to curse me, curse yourself and receive angelic slap, in the name of Jesus.

168. O God, arise and bring me out of the room that does not favour my destiny, in the name of Jesus.

Day 7 (15-08-21) - *The Bible in 70 Days (Day 7 - Exod 39:6 - Lev 1:1-14:3)*
Devotional Songs (Pages 4-10)
Praise and Worship
Prayers of Praise and Thanksgiving (Page 13)

169. Anyone hunting my life for destruction, be consumed by fire, in Jesus' name.

170. What I can use to conquer the enemies, O Lord, give it to me, in Jesus' name.

171. O God, bring me out of the covenant of my family idol, in Jesus' name.

172. O God, arise and let Your fire pursue my enemies to their graves, in the name of Jesus.

173. Every grave cloth covering my blessings, catch fire, in the name of Jesus.

174. Powers negotiating revenge concerning me, let them be wasted, in the name of Jesus.

175. O God my Father, let all my pursuers labour in vain, in the name of Jesus.

176. Any power sponsoring my suffering, be wasted, in the name of Jesus.

177. Every mouth that says living will not be easy for me, receive angelic slap, in the name of Jesus.

178. Powers fighting my story not to change, lose your power over me, in the name of Jesus.

179. Every battle facing me that is beyond my wisdom, O God, release Your fire to swallow it, in the name of Jesus.

180. Wicked powers drying up the well of my glory, become paralysed by fire, in the name of Jesus.

181. Evil anointed words fighting against me, backfire, in the name of Jesus.

182. Enemies rejoicing over my tears, receive the arrow of death, in Jesus' name.

183. Agreement of the wicked elders to deal with me, arrow of God, confuse it, in the name of Jesus.

184. Every strange gap between me and my place of joy, close by fire, in the name of Jesus.

185. Every power contributing battle to my problems, carry your load and die, in the name of Jesus.

186. Wicked prayers, my life is not available for you, backfire, in Jesus' name.

187. Egg of the wicked elders laid in my destiny, catch fire, in the name of Jesus.

188. What the enemy wants me to become will make them cry, in Jesus' name.

189. Powers desperately looking for my blood, be wasted in your own blood, in the name of Jesus.

190. Powers using my image to control me for destruction, thunder of God, strike them to death, in the name of Jesus.

191. Blood of Jesus, silence the blood of the wicked crying against me, in the name of Jesus.

192. Every battle that has come to stay in my life, consuming fire of God, swallow it, in the name of Jesus.

193. O God, arise and send Your thunder to strike the chariots of the enemy gathered against me, in the name of Jesus.

194. Every iron of affliction assigned against my life, be broken, in Jesus' name.

195. Iron bondage taking me far away from my joy, break and release me, in the name of Jesus.

196. O God, arise and put my stubborn enemies to perpetual sleep, in the name of Jesus.

Day 8 (16-08-21) - *The Bible in 70 Days (Day 8 - Lev 14:4 - 26:35)*
Devotional Songs (Pages 4-10)
Praise and Worship
Prayers of Praise and Thanksgiving (Page 13)

197. I fly over every mountain of failure and backwardness, in the name of Jesus.

198. O God my Father, break every oppression in my life, in the name of Jesus.

199. Powers, cursing my sun to go down, receive angelic slap, in Jesus' name.

200. Darkness that has covered my life, catch fire, in the name of Jesus.

201. The power of darkness that has arrested my morning, release it by fire, in the name of Jesus.

202. O God, arise and provoke my morning to favour my destiny, in Jesus' name.

203. O God, arise and let the light of my destiny break out from every darkness, in the name of Jesus.

204. Wicked gathering of the wicked elders aimed at stopping my morning, scatter by fire, in the name of Jesus.

205. Hand of the Almighty God, strengthen my hand, in the name of Jesus.

206. O God, arise and strengthen my hands to prosper, in the name of Jesus.

207. O God, arise and put me under the shadow of Your wings, in Jesus' name.

208. Anyone dragging my destiny ladder with me, run mad and die, in the name of Jesus.

209. The hole in the earth that will swallow my enemies alive, open now by fire, in the name of Jesus.

210. Powers holding the secret of my greatness, run mad and die, in Jesus' name.

211. Every power biting me in the secret, thunder of God, expose it and strike it to death, in the name of Jesus.

212. O God, arise and let Your angels recover all that the enemies have scattered in my destiny, in the name of Jesus.

213. Every finished work of darkness to make my life produce shame, scatter by fire, in the name of Jesus.

214. Where the enemy is expecting me to be a slave, O Lord, make me a king, in the name of Jesus.

215. Anyone using the words of his mouth to put me in bondage, receive angelic slap, in the name of Jesus.

216. Authority for great change, come upon my life, in the name of Jesus.

217. Every chain hindering my story from changing, break away from me, in the name of Jesus.

218. Every curse that has stolen from me, break and restore what you have stolen, in the name of Jesus.

219. Every good thing that the wicked elders have snatched away from me through manipulation, I recover it by fire, in the name of Jesus.

220. Powers using my picture to steal from me, die, in the name of Jesus.

221. Wicked elders assigned to issue curses to snatch my blessings from me, O God arise, snatch away their peace, in the name of Jesus.

222. Every curse being sent at the edge of my blessings, backfire, in Jesus' name.

223. Powers using curses to dominate my day, receive the arrow of death, in the name of Jesus.

224. Dark powers imposing on me the battle that is not mine, carry your load and die, in the name of Jesus.

Day 9 (17-08-21) - *The Bible in 70 Days (Day 9 - Lev 26:36 - Num 1:1-10:16)*
Devotional Songs (Pages 4-10)
Praise and Worship
Prayers of Praise and Thanksgiving (Page 13)

225. O God, arise and let the bitterness the enemy wants for me to manifest in his life, in the name of Jesus.

226. O God, arise and snatch the joy of the evil man expecting evil to happen to me, in the name of Jesus.

227. Any evil message left in my house by dark powers, scatter by fire, in the name of Jesus.

PRAYER BATTLE (2)

228. Powers sent to imprison my destiny, you are failures, die, in Jesus' name.

229. Light of God, arise and enter my home, in the name of Jesus.

230. Evil spiritual food prepared against my destiny, catch fire, in Jesus' name.

231. Every tongue commanding destruction against me, be condemned, in the name of Jesus.

232. Every spirit of death hunting my life, catch fire, in the name of Jesus.

233. Dark powers assigned to whip me to death, die with your instrument, in the name of Jesus.

234. My life, I wrestle you from the hand of untimely death, in the name of Jesus.

235. Blood of Jesus, wipe out my name from the book of darkness, in Jesus' name.

236. Wicked powers commanding me into untimely grave, receive angelic slap, in the name of Jesus.

237. Every grave molesting my existence, catch fire, in the name of Jesus.

238. Every wickedness around me, scatter by fire, in the name of Jesus.

239. Storm of darkness blocking my testimony, clear away by fire, in Jesus' name.

240. Rain of darkness multiplying evil plants in my destiny, stop now, in the name of Jesus.

241. Anyone having evil mind against my destiny, fire of God, consume him now, in the name of Jesus.

242. Anyone declaring that my storm will not be over, receive angelic slap, in the name of Jesus.

243. Powers cursing me to keep falling into trouble, die, in the name of Jesus.

244. Days of terror waiting to manifest in my life, expire, in the name of Jesus.

245. Any power boasting that I will cry whenever I am supposed to laugh, receive the arrow of death, in the name of Jesus.

246. O God, let Your mercy cease upon my enemies, in the name of Jesus.

247. Fear of failure hunting my life, die, in the name of Jesus.

248. Spirit of wickedness that has refused to let me go, die, in the name of Jesus.

249. O Lord, let the path of my enemy be slippery, in the name of Jesus.

250. Powers cheating on my destiny, O God, arise and judge them quickly, in the name of Jesus.

251. Where my glory is being cheated, O God, arise and fight for me, in the name of Jesus.

252. Every wicked concoction that I have drunk, that is affecting my destiny, expire by fire, in the name of Jesus.

Day 10 (18-08-21) - *The Bible in 70 Days (Day 10 - Num 10:17 - 24:3)*

Devotional Songs (Pages 4-10)
Praise and Worship
Prayers of Praise and Thanksgiving (Page 13)

253. Every hand that has hindered my destiny from having a meaning, catch fire, in the name of Jesus.

254. Powers using my life to do evil wonders, receive the arrow of destruction, in the name of Jesus.

255. Blood of Jesus, protect me from the touch of evil animals, in Jesus' name.

256. Every satanic animal declaring war against me, I overcome you now by the blood of Jesus, in the name of Jesus.

257. Every demonic animal assigned to put me back in bondage, catch fire, in the name of Jesus.

258. Powers demanding for my destiny, catch fire, in the name of Jesus.

259. Every spirit of the dog in me, catch fire, in the name of Jesus.

260. Every head of strange serpent rising against me, catch fire, in Jesus' name.

261. The good things that are at the point of death in my life, receive life now, in the name of Jesus.

262. Evil snake crawling around my destiny, dry up and die, in the name of Jesus.

263. Any herbalist using animals to attack me, harm yourself to death, in the name of Jesus.

264. Anything in my life, that the power of captivity is using against me, come out by fire, in the name of Jesus.

265. Powers introducing problems to me every month, be wasted now, in the name of Jesus.

266. Every bondage of death against me, scatter by fire, in the name of Jesus.

267. Powers tormenting me with depression, die suddenly, in the name of Jesus.

268. Demonic storm raging violently against me, come to an end now, in the name of Jesus.

269. Powers that want my loved ones to cry because of me, receive the arrow of death, in the name of Jesus.

270. Spirit of madness sent to disgrace me, die, in the name of Jesus.

271. Spirit of slavery and begging disgracing my destiny, die, in Jesus' name.

272. Wicked elders monitoring me from different angles, die in frustration, in the name of Jesus.

273. Every property of the enemy in my destiny, catch fire, in the name of Jesus.

274. O God, arise and catch my enemies by the hand and let them release my blessings, in the name of Jesus.

275. Powers that have vowed to live long on my sufferings, Lion of the tribe of Judah, jump on them and consume them, in the name of Jesus.

276. Powers punishing my destiny as if I don't know how to pray, run mad and die, in the name of Jesus.

277. Powers making me to suffer and have vowed never to leave me, O God, arise and judge them quickly, in the name of Jesus.

278. Powers that have vowed to make frustration my food, O God, arise and beat them to death, in the name of Jesus.

279. Powers that are boasting that they would see how God will save me, O God, arise and bury them, in the name of Jesus.

280. Power pointing arrows at me to make me hate myself, swallow your arrows and die, in the name of Jesus.

SECTION CONFESSIONS

I tread upon and destroy completely, all strongholds and barriers of the enemy against me, in the name of Jesus. I tread on them with the shoes of the gospel of the Lord Jesus Christ. I make an utter ruin of them all and all their possessions, kingdoms, thrones, dominions, palaces and everything in them, in Jesus' name. I erase them all and I make them completely desolate, in Jesus' name. My strength is in the Lord Jesus Christ. Jesus is my strength; I receive strength from the Lord, in the name of Jesus. The word of God says that He will restore to me, the years that the locust has eaten, the cankerworm, and the caterpillar, and the palmerworm, in the name of Jesus. With the blood of Jesus, the Lord will flush my land and wash my palms and possessions, in the name of Jesus. The whole world may decide to go wild with evil flowing like a flood. The enemy, in his evil machinations, may decide against me. The earth may choose not to tremble; whatever may be or happen, I refuse to be shaken, in the name of Jesus.

Who is like unto Him, our God, who dwells on high, far above all powers and dominions? He raiseth up the poor out of the dust, and lifteth the needy out of the dunghill; that He might set him with princes. Even so, shall the Lord deal with me, in the name of Jesus. The Bible says, whatsoever I desire when I pray, I should believe and receive, in the name of Jesus. Therefore, I pray now that, in Jesus' name, I am set free from every captivity or attack of negative speech from my mouth or thoughts and from my heart, against myself. I tear down, in faith, every spiritual wall of partition, between me and my divinely appointed helpers and benefactors, in the name of Jesus.

SECTION VIGIL

(To be done at night between the hours of 12 midnight and 2am)

HYMN FOR THE VIGIL (Pages 10-11)

1. Arrows that stole from me, be broken by the power of God, in Jesus' name.

2. Any power assigned to bury the legs of my enemies in my leg, die, in the name of Jesus.

3. Spiritual worms assigned to destroy my life gradually, come out and die, in the name of Jesus.

4. Any grave holding my feet captive, scatter, in the name of Jesus.

5. The expectation of evil over my life by the enemy shall never manifest, in the name of Jesus.

6. Satanic expectation over my life, refuse to manifest, in the name of Jesus.

7. Every evil success over my life, terminate, in the name of Jesus.

PRAYER BATTLE (2)

8. Powers that are going to prepare for battle over my case, I bury you now, in the name of Jesus.

9. Powers, fighting me from within, destroy yourselves, in the name of Jesus.

10. Any power that has gone to secure evil power to destroy me, I destroy you, in the name of Jesus.

11. O God, arise and pass through the hiding places of the enemy with Your fire, in the name of Jesus.

12. Evil eyes scanning my life, go blind, in the name of Jesus.

13. Any evil material used for me as a baby cloth, fire of God, locate it and destroy it, in the name of Jesus.

14. I cut off every evil hand on the affairs of my life, in the name of Jesus.

15. I shall not be a target; I shall not be wearied and I shall not be afflicted any longer, in the name of Jesus.

16. Any satanic incantation used to tie down my journey with slow motion, scatter, in the name of Jesus.

17. I cut off every hand attacking my daily benefits and my rewards, in the name of Jesus.

18. The battle of 'work very hard, but have little result', die, in the name of Jesus.

19. Every hand assigned to pull me down, wither, in the name of Jesus.

20. Powers assigned to reduce me from my level, die, in the name of Jesus.

21. Every utterance of backwardness, targeted at me, backfire, in Jesus' name.

SECTION 2 - THOU ART MY BATTLE AXE

Scripture Reading: 1 Samuel 17

Confession: Jeremiah 51:20 Thou art my battle axe and weapons of war: for with thee will I break in pieces the nations, and with thee will I destroy kingdoms;

Day 1 (19-08-21) - *The Bible in 70 Days (Day 11 - Num 24:4 - Deut 1:1-2)*

Devotional Songs (Pages 4-10)

Praise and Worship

Prayers of Praise and Thanksgiving (Page 13)

1. Forces terrorising my destiny, be consumed by fire, in the name of Jesus.

2. O God, arise and provoke my enemies to give up on me, in the name of Jesus.

3. Powers using my destiny for evil business, Rock of Ages, grind them to powder, in the name of Jesus.

4. Powers marking me for evil, catch fire, in the name of Jesus.

5. Anything in my life making me powerless before the enemy, O God, arise and kill it, in the name of Jesus.

6. Wherever I have been sold to by the enemy, blood of Jesus, buy me back, in the name of Jesus.

7. Powers assigned to make me a carrier of evil magnet, burn to ashes, in the name of Jesus.

8. Any wicked herbalist adding to my battles, run mad and die, in Jesus' name.

9. Any herbalist sent to wage war against me, wage war against yourself, in the name of Jesus.

10. Dark judgement against my life, scatter by fire, in the name of Jesus.

11. Powers preparing shame for me, die with your shame, in the name of Jesus.

12. Every bar of darkness blocking my way, scatter by fire, in the name of Jesus.

13. Powers that say nothing good will ever come out of me, die, in Jesus' name.

14. Powers blocking my eyes from the solution to my problems, be disappointed, in the name of Jesus.

15. Powers assigned to turn me to a slave before my enemies, receive the arrow of death, in the name of Jesus.

16. Powers placing an arrow of self-destruction in my hands, carry your load and die, in the name of Jesus.

17. Powers planning to destroy my name before my helpers, run mad, in the name of Jesus.

18. Eyes of the wicked following me about, catch fire, in the name of Jesus.

19. Gathering of the wicked assigned to make me their slave, thunder of God, scatter it, in the name of Jesus.

20. Garment of falling and not rising again, sewn for me, catch fire, in Jesus' name.

21. Powers pressing my head to the ground, receive the arrow of death, in the name of Jesus.

22. Strangers representing me to implicate me, fire of God, consume them, in the name of Jesus.

23. Every strange secret that the enemy is using as a weapon against me, O God, arise and scatter it, in the name of Jesus.

24. Every secret that I do not know, and that has become a battle for me, expire, in the name of Jesus.

25. The arrow the enemies have shot against me, that is yet to manifest, scatter by fire, in the name of Jesus.

26. Evil secret of the enemy that is giving him an advantage over me, be exposed and be disgraced, in the name of Jesus.

27. The secret of the wicked elders that is gradually killing my destiny, be terminated now, in the name of Jesus.

28. The secret that wicked elders know about my life, to put it in bondage, blood of Jesus, scatter it, in the name of Jesus.

Day 2 (20-08-21) - *The Bible in 70 Days (Day 12 -Deuteronomy 1:3 - 15:20)*
Devotional Songs (Pages 4-10)
Praise and Worship
Prayers of Praise and Thanksgiving (Page 13)

29. Powers using the secret that I do not know to increase my problem, O God, arise and disappoint them, in the name of Jesus.

30. Every secret strengthening my enemies against me, O Lord, kill it, in the name of Jesus.

31. Powers holding the key of my room that contains what will make me great, release it to me by fire, in the name of Jesus.

32. Every secret garment of battle that the enemy has put on me to stop me from rising, catch fire, in the name of Jesus.

33. Every secret prayer of the enemy dragging my life backward, die by fire, in the name of Jesus.

34. Every secret prayer of the enemy making failure my name, be terminated now, in the name of Jesus.

35. Secret agents of darkness working hard to make me cry, be wasted by fire, in the name of Jesus.

36. Secret smell of darkness driving my helpers away, blood of Jesus, clear it away, in the name of Jesus.

37. Every secret favour that unfriendly friends have got from the wicked elders to put me to shame, become a trap of death for them, in the name of Jesus.

38. Lord, let the secret weapon of darkness frustrating my effort become their trap of death, in the name of Jesus.

39. Powers cursing me to make mistakes to uncover my nakedness, die, in the name of Jesus.

40. Battles assigned to embarrass me in front of those who should celebrate me, scatter by fire, in the name of Jesus.

41. Every strange mess assigned to embarrass me before my enemies, blood of Jesus, wipe it away, in the name of Jesus.

42. Evil joining of hands and legs to kill what will make me to be celebrated, dry up by fire, in the name of Jesus.

43. Arrow of God, arise and deliver me from the battle facing me, in Jesus' name.

44. O God, arise and surprise my enemies with Your arrow, in the name of Jesus.

45. Terrible arrow of God, descend on the coven of darkness making wicked decisions against me, in the name of Jesus.

46. O God, let Your arrow cause my enemies to fall under me, in Jesus' name.

47. Lord, let all that my enemies rely on against me become their grave, in the name of Jesus.

PRAYER BATTLE (2)

48. O God, arise and let Your mighty weapon silence my storm, in Jesus' name.

49. O God, spare not Your arrow against my wicked enemies, in the name of Jesus.

50. Arrows of God, destroy the hiding place of my enemies where charms are stored against me, in the name of Jesus.

51. O God, arise and cut off every wicked tongue against me, in the name of Jesus.

52. Every tongue of the wicked assigned to tear me down, catch fire, in the name of Jesus.

53. Tongues of the wicked elders against me, receive the judgement of death, in the name of Jesus.

54. Deception of the wicked elders assigned to put my life in bondage, expire, in the name of Jesus.

55. Powers consulting the dead to curse my destiny, run mad and die, in the name of Jesus.

56. Powers using me as an instrument of covenant in their evil group, receive the judgement of death, in the name of Jesus.

Day 3 (21-08-21) - *Reading the Bible in 70 Days (Day 13- Deut. 15:21- 32:26)*
Devotional Songs (Pages 4-10)
Praise and Worship
Prayers of Praise and Thanksgiving (Page 13)

57. O God, arise and bring me out of the pit of trouble, in the name of Jesus.

58. Every fire of trouble burning in every area of my life, I quench you, in the name of Jesus.

59. Every evil mouth calling troubles into my life, receive angelic slaps, in the name of Jesus.

60. Repeated trouble rising anytime I am at the edge of breakthrough, die, in the name of Jesus.

61. Sudden trouble assigned to trouble my life, scatter by fire, in Jesus' name.

62. Every long time stubborn trouble, troubling my destiny, expire, in Jesus' name.

63. Arrow of acidic trouble fired at me, backfire, in the name of Jesus.

64. Trap of trouble from the pit of hell, you shall not catch me, die, in Jesus' name.

65. Atmosphere of trouble around me, fade away by fire, in the name of Jesus.

PRAYER BATTLE (2)

66. Those who rejoice to see me in trouble shall regret very soon, in Jesus' name.

67. I refuse to buy trouble with my money, in the name of Jesus.

68. Future trap of trouble prepared against me, scatter by fire, in Jesus' name.

69. Holy Spirit, drain out the flood of trouble from my destiny, in Jesus' name.

70. Incantation of trouble hanging in the air against me, be consumed by fire, in the name of Jesus.

71. Every power that says I will not rest from trouble, die, in the name of Jesus.

72. Rain of troubles, soak the life of my enemies, in the name of Jesus.

73. Every satanic lie and liars fashioned against my destiny, be terminated now, in the name of Jesus.

74. Strange covenants that have sold my life to troubles, break by fire, in the name of Jesus.

75. Secret joy of the enemy over my life, scatter by fire, in the name of Jesus.

76. Battle of the grave that is making me restless, scatter by fire, in Jesus' name.

77. Tree of death growing against my destiny, catch fire, in the name of Jesus.

78. Arrows assigned to make me sleep in disgrace and wake up in nakedness, backfire, in the name of Jesus.

79. Battles secretly wounding my destiny, scatter by fire, in the name of Jesus.

80. Powers pretending to have authority over my life and destiny, collapse and die, in the name of Jesus.

81. O God, arise and release Your tongue of fire upon the enemies that are planning disaster for me, in the name of Jesus.

82. Spirit of the grave sent to swallow me, swallow your sender, in Jesus' name.

83. Wicked elders planning sorrowful condition for me, die, in the name of Jesus.

84. Sword of darkness sent against me, backfire without affecting me, in the name of Jesus.

Day 4 (22-08-21) - *The Bible in 70 Days (Day 14 - Deut 32:27 - Jos 1:1- 15:27)*
Devotional Songs (Pages 4-10)
Praise and Worship
Prayers of Praise and Thanksgiving (Page 13)

85. Powers selling my glory in the house of darkness, run mad, in Jesus' name.

PRAYER BATTLE (2)

86. Wicked powers that want my glory to die by mistake, you are failures, die suddenly, in the name of Jesus.

87. Fire of darkness, assigned to burn my destiny to ashes, be quenched suddeny, in the name of Jesus.

88. Every battle growing against me, be wasted, in the name of Jesus.

89. The mark the evil elders put on me to track down my destiny, blood of Jesus wipe it off, in the name of Jesus.

90. Demonic number identifying me for destruction, catch fire, in Jesus' name.

91. The odour that the wicked elders have put on me, for their agents to identify me for battle, expire, in the name of Jesus.

92. Strange hand assisting the wicked elders to locate me, catch fire, in the name of Jesus.

93. Powers that cursed the day of my birth, O God, tear them to pieces, in the name of Jesus.

94. Arrow of darkness that has stayed too long in my life, catch fire, in the name of Jesus.

95. The battle my parents fought and could not overcome, I overcome you by fire, in the name of Jesus.

96. Powers that say "as long as tomorrow does not end, my battle will not end", receive the stone of death, in the name of Jesus.

97. Lord, let the strange mountain the enemy is climbing against me crumble, in the name of Jesus.

98. Wicked powers helping themselves against me, destroy yourselves, in the name of Jesus.

99. Anointing of evil confession against me, dry up now, in the name of Jesus.

100. Evil strangers assigned to attack me unawares, receive the arrow of death, in the name of Jesus.

101. Every power cursing my day, O God, arise and silence it in the grave forever, in the name of Jesus.

102. Ancient of Days, destroy the ancient battle that is silently wasting my blessings, in the name of Jesus.

103. Multiple birds of darkness assigned to announce my obituary, be consumed by fire, in the name of Jesus.

104. Dark powers saying it is an abomination for me to see the favour of God, lose your power over me, in the name of Jesus.

105. Dark powers locking me up in the darkroom of battle, leave me alone and die, in the name of Jesus.

106. Powers stealing from me to sponsor battle against me, receive the judgement of death, in the name of Jesus.

107. I shall not swallow the pill of death, by the power in the blood of Jesus, in the name of Jesus.

108. Powers assigned to donate me as food for the dining table of darkness, Lion of the tribe of Judah, tear them to pieces, in the name of Jesus.

109. Deadly power, hear the word of the Lord, I have no case to answer, reverse your step and be consumed by fire, in the name of Jesus.

110. Appetite of the grave, my family and I are not your meat, die, in Jesus' name.

111. Powers that entered into evil contract against my life, die, in Jesus' name.

112. Ritual of darkness carried out to waste me, catch fire, in the name of Jesus.

Day 5 (23-08-21) *The Bible in 70 Days (Day 15-Jos 15:28-24:33; Jud 1:1- 6:20)*
Devotional Songs (Pages 4-10)
Praise and Worship
Prayers of Praise and Thanksgiving (Page 13)

113. Powers using dark prayers to drag me down, run mad and die, in the name of Jesus.

114. Powers using strange words to kill my joy, I silence you by fire, in the name of Jesus.

115. Powers assigned to make me suffer from deadly mistakes, be frustrated and die, in the name of Jesus.

116. Powers assigned to quench the light of my glory, die, in the name of Jesus.

117. O Lord, let the company of wasteful men in my destiny scatter, in the name of Jesus.

118. Wicked elders assigned to flood my life with troubles, O God, arise and judge

them quickly, in the name of Jesus.

119. Wicked powers faking evil cry to attract favour to destroy me, receive the sword of death, in the name of Jesus.

120. Powers wearing rags to see that my life is destroyed, destroy yourselves, in the name of Jesus.

121. Battles assigned to see that I do not have rest till I die, be terminated quickly, in the name of Jesus.

122. Every storm of trouble sent against me, backfire, in the name of Jesus.

123. Wicked elders tormenting me and frustrating my efforts to get favour, O God, arise and judge them quickly, in the name of Jesus.

124. My enemies, hear the word of the Lord, carry all my load of problems by fire, in the name of Jesus.

125. Arrows that have been fired to steal from me, be broken by the power of God, in the name of Jesus.

126. Powers of the wicked elders behind my present situation, lose your hold over me, in the name of Jesus.

127. Wicked powers pursuing my blood to prolong their lives, be wasted in your own blood, in the name of Jesus.

128. Anyone pursuing my life for emergency sacrifices, receive the arrow of instant death, in the name of Jesus.

129. O God, arise and make me see Your punishment and judgement on my enemies, in the name of Jesus.

130. O God, arise and release shame on those scheming to put me to shame, in the name of Jesus.

131. Anyone allied to the devil against me, thunder of God, strike him to death, in the name of Jesus.

132. I receive the teeth of fire to thresh every mountain of problems in my life, in the name of Jesus.

133. Teeth of the enemy waiting to poison my success, I crush you to powder, in the name of Jesus.

134. Teeth of chronic poverty prepared against my prosperity, begin to bite your

owners now, in the name of Jesus.

135. Blood of Jesus, fight against the evil blood working against me, in the name of Jesus.

136. Every charm assigned to divert me from my place of destiny, catch fire, in the name of Jesus.

137. Crown of battle prepared for my head, backfire, in the name of Jesus.

138. Arrow fired at my destiny to make me live a desert life, scatter by fire, in the name of Jesus.

139. O God, arise and withdraw my food from my enemies, in the name of Jesus.

140. O God, arise and force my enemies to swallow the arrows they prepared for me, in the name of Jesus.

Day 6 (24-08-21) - *The Bible in 70 Days (Day 16 - Judges 6:21 - 21:17)*
Devotional Songs (Pages 4-10)
Praise and Worship
Prayers of Praise and Thanksgiving (Page 13)

141. Every evil power appearing through a dog against me, catch fire, in the name of Jesus.

142. Powers appointing me to be a carrier of evil problems, run mad and die, in the name of Jesus.

143. Powers assigned to mess up the grace of God upon my life, die, in the name of Jesus.

144. Powers that made my life sorrowful and that have refused to leave me alone, release me and die, in the name of Jesus.

145. Powers making it hard for me to celebrate, die, in the name of Jesus.

146. Where my strength cannot take me to, O God, arise and take me there, in the name of Jesus.

147. O God, arise and waste every power assigned to use strange sickness to waste my life, in the name of Jesus.

148. Powers assigned to pass through the pandemic to sacrifice my life, O God, disappoint them, in the name of Jesus.

149. O God, arise and let my enemies feed on their own blood, in Jesus' name.

PRAYER BATTLE (2)

150. Stones of death, locate the powers robbing me of my destiny, in the name of Jesus.

151. Powers using my life to prove their worth against my destiny, be wasted, in the name of Jesus.

152. Powers rewriting my destiny for sickness and death, be destroyed by fire, in the name of Jesus.

153. Evil circle of problems disturbing my life, break away from me by fire, in the name of Jesus.

154. O God, arise and deliver me from all the battles of life assigned to take my life, in the name of Jesus.

155. Anything that will drag me to an untimely death shall not be my choice, in the name of Jesus.

156. Holy Spirit, strike all those who seek to harm my family with blindness, in the name of Jesus.

157. All those who go about consulting mediums, false prophets, enchanters and powers of darkness to inquire about me, destroy yourselves, in Jesus' name.

158. O Lord, I know that You can do everything. Protect me and my family from the dangers of the world, in the name of Jesus.

159. O God, arise and remove pains and bitterness from my destiny, in the name of Jesus.

160. O God, arise and withdraw my destiny from the hands of wicked slave masters, in the name of Jesus.

161. O Lord, destroy the shield covering my enemies, in the name of Jesus.

162. O Lord, reveal the powers behind my battle and consume them, in the name of Jesus.

163. Evil hands pointed at me to change my destiny, O Lord, set them ablaze, in the name of Jesus.

164. You, enemy of my long life, stay far away from me, in the name of Jesus.

165. O Lord, let everything that gives my enemies strength and joy to attack me disappear by fire, in the name of Jesus.

166. Every power meeting evil prophets to increase my confusion, die, in the

PRAYER BATTLE (2)

name of Jesus.

167. Secret battles fighting against me, go back to your senders, in Jesus' name.

168. Powers secretly killing my star, run mad, in the name of Jesus.

Day 7 (25-08-21) - *Bible in 70 Days (Day 17 - Jud 21:18 - 1Sam 1:1- 15:4)*
Devotional Songs (Pages 4-10)
Praise and Worship
Prayers of Praise and Thanksgiving (Page 13)

169. Holy Ghost, disconnect me from deadly enemies, in the name of Jesus.

170. Trap of strange sickness sent against me, terminate your owner, in the name of Jesus.

171. Anyone secretly making himself available to be used by satan to destroy me, be paralysed, in the name of Jesus.

172. I collect my pot of blessings that the enemies are hiding from me back by fire, in the name of Jesus.

173. Wicked elders coming close to me to conclude their wicked works over my life, receive the arrows of death, in the name of Jesus.

174. Secret curse of the elders wasting my existence, break by fire, in the name of Jesus.

175. I release my prosperity from the hands of my jealous enemies, in the name of Jesus.

176. Every jealous power raging against me, run mad, in the name of Jesus.

177. O God, turn the wisdom of my enemies against me to their coffin, in the name of Jesus.

178. Powers attacking my grace, be wasted, in the name of Jesus.

179. Every hidden enemy diverting all my blessings, be terminated, in the name of Jesus.

180. O Lord, use whoever is afflicting me to create a great way for me, in the name of Jesus.

181. Any problem that came into my life through a strange wind, die by fire, in the name of Jesus.

182. O God, let the world identify my tormentors with reproach, in Jesus' name.

PRAYER BATTLE (2)

183. O God, arise and let peace of mind be scarce in the life of my wicked enemies, in the name of Jesus.

184. Powers using my glory to survive, be suddenly wasted, in the name of Jesus.

185. My next breakthroughs will silence all my enemies and destroy their works against me, in the name of Jesus.

186. O Lord, destroy the enemies of my freedom, in the name of Jesus.

187. Arrow of the enemies that has been working against me without stopping, catch fire, in the name of Jesus.

188. The enemies working hard to afflict my destiny with battles, die, in the name of Jesus.

189. Curse of the Lord, locate those who are bent on pushing me out of the track of my blessings, in the name of Jesus.

190. Any defilement assigned to pull me down, expire with your content, in the name of Jesus.

191. Curse of the Lord, kill all those dragging me away from heavenly security, in the name of Jesus.

192. Curse of the Lord, destroy those that want my greener pastures to fade, in the name of Jesus.

193. Curse of the Lord, swallow all those that want me to be seen and be rejected by people, in the name of Jesus.

194. Curse of the Lord, silence the war cry of the enemies over my destiny, in the name of Jesus.

195. Curse of the Lord, tear the throat of the enemy drinking the blood of my glory like water, in the name of Jesus.

196. Any dark power running errand of wickedness for my sake, reap double destruction, in the name of Jesus.

Day 8 (26-08-21) - *The Bible in 70 Days (Day 18 -1Samuel 15:5 - 30:31)*
Devotional Songs (Pages 4-10)
Praise and Worship
Prayers of Praise and Thanksgiving (Page 13)

197. The valley of the shadow of death shall not consume me on the day of my joy, in the name of Jesus.

198. My eyes shall not go blind on the day of my joy. My ears shall not be deaf on the day of my joy; and my mouth shall not be dumb on the day of my joy, in the name of Jesus.

199. Battles of life that have no respect for anyone, you shall not swallow me and my family, in the name of Jesus.

200. Battles stopping me from becoming somebody, disappear from my life, in the name of Jesus.

201. Battles assigned to write me off when it remains a day for me to be celebrated, scatter, in the name of Jesus.

202. Heat of darkness assigned to strangulate my destiny, clear away by fire, in the name of Jesus.

203. Strange strength of the enemy terrorising my freedom, be drained by the Holy Ghost fire, in the name of Jesus.

204. O God, visit the emergency situation in my life and make me laugh last over my enemies, in the name of Jesus.

205. O God, deliver me completely from the challenges facing me as if there is no God to deliver, in the name of Jesus.

206. O Lord, stain my enemies with their blood of regret, in the name of Jesus.

207. O Lord, tear down the great foundation of my enemies, in Jesus' name.

208. Glory of God, overshadow my life and let it make sense before You, in the name of Jesus.

209. As the enemy has made the favour of God to run away from me, O Lord, lift me up by Your mercy and power, in the name of Jesus.

210. Strange blood in my hands, be washed off by the blood of Jesus, in the name of Jesus.

211. Father, fight every war dedicated against me by my enemies, in Jesus' name.

212. Any power using strange breast to programme evil against me, die, in the name of Jesus.

213. Anyone carrying sacrifice against me at night and waiting to hear bad news about me, fire of God, destroy him unawares, in the name of Jesus.

214. Any long-staying arrow in my life, pack your load and get out, in the name

of Jesus.

215. Every arrow diverting my blessings to someone else in the village, backfire, in the name of Jesus.

216. Strong man that is interested in destroying my destiny because of what God is doing in my life, fall down and die, in the name of Jesus.

217. Arrows that usually steal from me, be broken by fire, in the name of Jesus.

218. Strange spiritual garment, fall away from my body, in the name of Jesus.

219. Any arrow that wants to turn me to a shameful beggar, scatter by fire, in the name of Jesus.

220. Powers using my late relation to swallow my virtues, catch fire, in the name of Jesus.

221. O Lord, remove every bad habit in my life that is causing problem to others, in the name of Jesus.

222. My Father, send any man/woman to me that will help fulfil my destiny without adding any sorrow to it, in the name of Jesus.

223. My destiny, you shall not disappoint God, in the name of Jesus.

224. Blood of Jesus, wipe out everything in me that is killing me, in Jesus' name.

Day 9(27-08-21) - *The Bible in 70 Days (Day 19 - 1Sam 31:1 - 2Sam 1:1-17:5)*
Devotional Songs (Pages 4-10)
Praise and Worship
Prayers of Praise and Thanksgiving (Page 13)

225. My hand, refuse to befriend poverty, in the name of Jesus.

226. With the blood of Jesus, I destroy every dream disgracing me, in the name of Jesus.

227. Evil flies of the enemies following me like a shadow, catch fire, in the name of Jesus.

228. O Lord, let my enemies lick the dust in disgrace, in the name of Jesus.

229. My mistakes from the past, making me wear curse like a garment, blood of Jesus, scatter them, in the name of Jesus.

230. Holy Ghost, flog the enemies of my progress till they take their hands off, in the name of Jesus.

PRAYER BATTLE (2)

231. O Lord, if I have left my place of blessings, chase me back there, in the name of Jesus.

232. Lord, let my enemies prostrate to me in tears, in the name of Jesus.

233. I rebuke and kill the spirit of satanic tiredness in my blood, in Jesus' name.

234. O Lord, kill stammering power in my tongue, in the name of Jesus.

235. My enemies that never cease to go to herbalists for help; O God, terminate them, in the name of Jesus.

236. O Lord, erase my physical and spiritual problem with ease, in Jesus' name.

237. All enemies running around to destroy me shall be a source of blessing for me, in the name of Jesus.

238. Whatever has been set up to do me harm, the Lord shall use it for my goodness, in the name of Jesus.

239. I speak destruction unto the headquarters of the wicked elders; and I blow up their altars, in the name of Jesus.

240. Ancestral graveyard of my father's house, waiting for my body in the grave, catch fire, in the name of Jesus.

241. By the power of God, I will not embark on the journey that will lead me to the mortuary, in the name of Jesus.

242. O Lord, let the water from the side of Christ wash away every poison in my life, in the name of Jesus.

243. All curses harassing my life, go back to where you came from and be replaced with blessings in my life, in the name of Jesus.

244. Sword of the Lord, pass through the camp of my enemies for destruction, in the name of Jesus.

245. My Father, send the horses and the riders assigned to trouble me into a deep sleep, in the name of Jesus.

246. Destructive rain of God, fall upon every violent battle arranged against me, in the name of Jesus.

247. O God, arise and send Your wasters to waste every enemy of my destiny, in the name of Jesus.

248. Wasters from heaven, waste every force of Goliath assigned against me, in

the name of Jesus.

249. Every power assigned to molest me, I command you to leave me forever, in the name of Jesus.

250. O Lord, by Your mercy, my ladder of greatness shall not break, in the name of Jesus.

251. Satanic violence set up against the mercy of God for my life, scatter by fire, in the name of Jesus.

252. Wicked powers delaying the manifestation of my divine mercy, be destroyed, in the name of Jesus.

Day 10 (28-08-21)-*The Bible in 70 Days (Day 20 - 2Sam 17:6- 1Kings 1:1-6:3)*
Devotional Songs (Pages 4-10)
Praise and Worship
Prayers of Praise and Thanksgiving (Page 13)

253. Enemy of my progress within and without, I have obtained the mercy of God. Therefore, die in shame, in the name of Jesus.

254. By the mercy of God, I receive supernatural breakthroughs, in Jesus' name.

255. Arrow of wickedness preventing my rain of mercy, be destroyed by fire, in the name of Jesus.

256. By the mercy of God, every valley in my life shall bring water, in Jesus' name.

257. By the mercy of God, I shall not see reproach, I shall not see shame, I shall not see disappointment, in the name of Jesus.

258. O Lord, give me comforting authority to enable me to achieve my goal, in the name of Jesus.

259. Inspiration of witchcraft in my family, be destroyed, in the name of Jesus.

260. All evil thoughts against me, Lord, turn them to good for me, in Jesus' name.

261. You spirit of death and hell, you have no document in my life, die, in the name of Jesus.

262. My enemies will not catch me in any area of my life, in the name of Jesus.

263. O Lord, in any area of my life, let not my life disgrace You, in Jesus' name.

264. I will not be a victim of failure and I will not bite my finger for any reason, in the name of Jesus.

265. I refuse to be a candidate of the spirit of amputation, in the name of Jesus.

266. Everyday of my life, I shall move to higher ground, in the name of Jesus.

267. Everyday of my life, I shall disgrace all my stubborn pursuers, in the name of Jesus.

268. O Lord, make me a power generator, in the name of Jesus.

269. Lord, let divine accuracy come into my life and operations, in Jesus' name.

270. Every false testimony against my life, be exposed and be crushed, in the name of Jesus.

271. Evil hands that have been working in the shadow for my downfall shall be used to raise me higher, in the name of Jesus.

272. O Lord, turn the curses of my enemies upon their own heads, in Jesus' name.

273. 'Spirit of beating-about-the-bush' without making result, release me and die, in the name of Jesus.

274. 'Follow-follow-spirit', using my shadow to track me, go blind and be paralysed, in the name of Jesus.

275. Thou 'power of go-slow', in my life, catch fire, in the name of Jesus.

276. 'Spirit of thou shall not shine', die, in the name of Jesus.

277. Every load of darkness that will not allow me to succeed, catch fire, in the name of Jesus.

278. Load of the wicked elders residing in my body, come out and catch fire, in the name of Jesus.

279. Every load of the wicked elders that has constituted evil on my head, go back to your senders, in the name of Jesus.

280. Fire of God, dry up all evil rivers keeping the source of my problems, in the name of Jesus.

SECTION CONFESSION

I trust in the Lord, and I am not leaning on my understanding. I fill my heart with the words of faith; I receive and speak the words of faith. The young lions do lack and suffer hunger; but I who seek the Lord God Almighty, shall not lack any good thing, in the name of Jesus. God is my Strong Rock and my House of Defence, in the name of Jesus. In the name of Jesus Christ, I hand over all my battles to the Lord Jesus Christ. The Lord fights for me and I hold my peace. The Lord has bowed down His righteous ears, to deliver me speedily, in the name of Jesus. I shall eat the riches of the Gentiles, and in their glory, I shall boast myself, and all shall see and shall acknowledge that I am the seed, which the Lord has blessed.

I shall no longer be disappointed, or fail at the edge of my desired miracles, success and victory, in the name of Jesus. It is written: Behold, I and the children whom the Lord has given me are for signs and for wonders in Israel from the Lord of hosts which dwelleth in mount Zion. I stand upon this infallible word of God and claim every letter of its promises, in the name of Jesus. I also covenant myself and my household onto the Lord: my fruits, I shall dedicate and surrender to the blessings and pleasures of God who has blessed me and banished my reproach forever, in the name of Jesus. The Lord is my light and my salvation, whom shall I fear? The Lord is the strength of my life; of whom shall I be afraid? When the wicked, even mine enemies and foes, come upon me to eat up my flesh, they stumbled and fell, in the name of Jesus.

SECTION VIGIL

(To be done at night between the hours of 12 midnight and 2 am)

HYMN FOR THE VIGIL (Pages 10-11)

1. O God, arise, set me free from the bondage of backwardness, in Jesus' name

2. O God, arise and let the horse and its rider fighting against me, enter into destruction, in the name of Jesus.

3. Powers assigned to make my strength fail, fall down and die, in Jesus' name.

4. O Lord, let the weapon of the enemy fashioned against me fight the enemy, in the name of Jesus.

5. Plantation of darkness, hear the word of the Lord, my body is not your hiding place, come out and die, in the name of Jesus.

6. Blood of Jesus, arise and heal my wounds, in the name of Jesus.

7. Battles that insist that I must be put to shame, backfire, in the name of Jesus.

8. Every evil fire set to burn me, I put you out, in the name of Jesus.

9. Glory wasting arrows in my body, come out, in the name of Jesus.

10. Any sudden arrow fired into my body, catch fire suddenly, in Jesus' name.

11. Doors of new glory open unto me this year, in the name of Jesus.

12. Vultures of my father's house, vultures of my mother's house, assigned to feed on my destiny, eat your flesh and drink your blood, in the name of Jesus.

13. O God, arise, shine Your light on my path and lead me to great people, in the name of Jesus.

14. Powers that refused to let me excel, fall down and die, in the name of Jesus.

15. Every mocking battle, hear the word of the Lord, fall down and die, in the name of Jesus.

16. Every enemy that looks like a wall of Jericho to my life, I pull you down, in the name of Jesus.

17. O God, arise and terrify the battles of my life, in the name of Jesus.

18. Every curse that appears as blessings, go back to your senders, in Jesus' name.

19. Any power that wants me to live in debt, fall down and die, in Jesus' name.

20. Every prophecy meant to scatter good things in my life, go back to your sender, in the name of Jesus.

21. Every evil hand placed upon my head in the market, I shake you off, in the name of Jesus.

SECTION 3 - BREAKING THE BREAKER

Scripture Reading: Isaiah 37

Confession: Micah 2:3 Therefore thus saith the LORD; Behold, against this family do I devise an evil, from which ye shall not remove your necks; neither shall ye go haughtily: for this time is evil.

Day 1 (29-08-21) - *The Bible in 70 Days (Day 21- 1Kings 6:4-18:3)*

Devotional Songs (Pages 4-10)

Praise and Worship

Prayers of Praise and Thanksgiving (Page 13)

1. Evil agreement between me and unclean animals, die, in the name of Jesus.

2. You the ground, become too hot for my enemies, in the name of Jesus.

3. Any animal rising up at the edge of my miracle, I bring the judgement of God upon you, in the name of Jesus.

4. Wicked elders that have rubbished my glory, run mad, in the name of Jesus.

5. Every situation becoming too hard on me, die, in the name of Jesus.

6. Anointing of disgrace upon my life, be turned to grace, in the name of Jesus.

7. Every demonic fruit designed to bring me shame, catch fire, in Jesus' name.

8. Spirit of error and mistake assigned to waste my life, die, in the name of Jesus.

9. Every evil tree draining my life, catch fire, in the name of Jesus.

10. Rage of dryness assigned against me, be silenced by fire, in the name of Jesus.

11. Battles dragging me away from the promised land, scatter by fire, in the name of Jesus.

12. O God, arise and save me from the teeth of the wicked, in the name of Jesus.

13. Terrible teeth, fearsome teeth, assigned to waste my destiny, bite your sender, in the name of Jesus.

14. Sharp tongue cursing my destiny, catch fire, in the name of Jesus.

15. Teeth of anguish designed to crush my destiny in sorrow, die, in Jesus' name.

16. Powers chewing my destiny, your time is up, die now, in the name of Jesus.

17. Cursing powers, hear the word of the Lord, lose your power over me, in the name of Jesus.

18. Serpentine tongue assigned against my destiny, catch fire, in Jesus' name.

19. I cut off the head of my secret enemies, in the name of Jesus.

20. Powers that want to push me down from the mountain of honour, die, in the name of Jesus.

21. Powers that want me to dance in disgrace, receive the arrow of death, in the name of Jesus.

22. By the power in the blood of Jesus, I shall not answer the call of shame, in the name of Jesus.

23. The problem tying my destiny down like an animal, scatter by fire, in the name of Jesus.

24. Battle of no progress and no change, be terminated by fire, in Jesus' name.

25. Angels of darkness keeping me in the prison-house of poverty, thunder of God, scatter them, in the name of Jesus.

26. Everything sent to hurt and harm me shall honour me and bow to me, in the name of Jesus.

27. Fire of God, deliver my hand from the heat of satanic pot, in the name of Jesus.

28. Satanic basket upon my hands, catch fire, in the name of Jesus.

Day 2 (30-08-21)-*The Bible in 70 Days (Day 22 -1Kings 18:4- 2Kings 1:1-9:33)*
Devotional Songs (Pages 4-10)
Praise and Worship
Prayers of Praise and Thanksgiving (Page 13)

29. Satanic pot upon my head, catch fire, in the name of Jesus.

30. Age-long bondage standing like captivity in my life, be terminated, in the name of Jesus.

31. Powers that are determined to bring evil to pass in my life, be wasted, in the name of Jesus.

32. Rope of darkness drawing my destiny back and downward, break, in the name of Jesus.

33. Buyers and sellers of blood, I render my blood too hot and bitter for your business, in the name of Jesus.

34. Anyone in my family warming up to suck my blood, die, in the name of Jesus.

35. Satanic blood festivals arranged against my family, expire by fire, in the name

of Jesus.

36. Every satanic tube and arrow buried in my blood, burn to ashes, in the name of Jesus.

37. Evil pots for collecting blood, scatter and burn to ashes, in the name of Jesus.

38. You this ground, you shall not drink my blood this year, in the name of Jesus.

39. The God that answers by fire, arise and make it impossible for my enemies to spill my blood this year, in the name of Jesus.

40. Hunters of my blood, the blood of Jesus cries against you to death, in the name of Jesus.

41. My blood shall not be sacrificed for solution to a strange problem, in the name of Jesus.

42. Evil meeting to spill my blood shall be a burial ceremony for my enemies, in the name of Jesus.

43. Powers using different faces to attack me in the dream, receive the arrow of destruction, in the name of Jesus.

44. Secret tree serving as a stronghold for my enemies, catch fire, in Jesus' name.

45. I crush the head of whoever has received an evil assignment to make me cry, in the name of Jesus.

46. Powers shedding blood to create difficulties for me, die, in the name of Jesus.

47. Whoever is sitting on the throne of iniquity and possessing my wealth, release it and die, in the name of Jesus.

48. O Lord, make me a mysterious wonder, where men say it is finished for me, in the name of Jesus.

49. Powers assigned to use my past mistakes to torment me, die, in Jesus' name.

50. Powers saying that I will end up a failure like my ancestors, die, in Jesus' name.

51. Battles that have vowed to see my end, scatter by fire, in the name of Jesus.

52. Every great problem in my life, receive a greater solution, in the name of Jesus.

53. Wicked powers of my ancestors, die, in the name of Jesus.

54. Battles assigned to swallow me at the point of my glory, scatter by fire, in the name of Jesus.

55. Battle of financial nakedness, release me and die, in the name of Jesus.

56. Powers pursuing my virtues away from me, die, in the name of Jesus.

Day 3 (31-08-21) - *The Bible in 70 Days (Day 23 - 2Kings 9:34-25:11)*
Devotional Songs (Pages 4-10)
Praise and Worship
Prayers of Praise and Thanksgiving (Page 13)

57. My destiny that has been sacrificed to idols, blood of Jesus, bring it back, in the name of Jesus.

58. Powers claiming my head for a satanic stranger, run mad, in the name of Jesus.

59. Wicked sacrifice assigned to mess up my glory, be consumed by fire, in the name of Jesus.

60. Powers that have vowed that I will always face storms, perish by fire, in the name of Jesus.

61. Powers closing my gate of breakthroughs, die, in the name of Jesus.

62. Powers tormenting my peace, die, in the name of Jesus.

63. Demonic presence irritating my angel of blessings, disappear by fire, in the name of Jesus.

64. Powers trapping my life with repeated battles, die, in the name of Jesus.

65. Every power that wants to see my corpse in disgrace, be disappointed, in the name of Jesus.

66. Destructive fire of God, answer the expectations of the wicked against me, in the name of Jesus.

67. Powers using the dead to raise a voice against me, die, in the name of Jesus.

68. Powers sending the dead to flog me, run mad and die, in the name of Jesus.

69. O God, arise and put my enemies into an everlasting trap, in Jesus' name.

70. Powers using the wind as a weapon to afflict me, storm of fire, swallow them, in the name of Jesus.

71. Every strange spirit and its sender tormenting me with problems, run into the judgement of death, in the name of Jesus.

72. Arrows of disfavour fired into my head, locate your sender, in Jesus' name.

73. Arrows of satanic anger fired into my life, backfire, in the name of Jesus.

74. Arrows of constant failure and backwardness, backfire, in the name of Jesus.

PRAYER BATTLE (2)

75. Arrows of hatred and rejection fired into my life, jump out now, in Jesus' name.

76. Prophet of darkness sending battles into my life, run mad and die, in the name of Jesus.

77. Strange voice that says I will never wake up to my dream, I silence you by fire, in the name of Jesus.

78. Powers sending bullets to pull off my glory, be disappointed, in Jesus' name.

79. Every satanic punishment meted out to me, backfire, in the name of Jesus.

80. Powers using witchcraft to attack me, let your witchcraft backfire, in the name of Jesus.

81. Spiritual bullets of wicked powers fired against me, catch fire, in Jesus' name.

82. Waster of destiny eyeing my life, be wasted, in the name of Jesus.

83. I cancel evil arrangement designed to kill me, in the name of Jesus.

84. Every evil water poured into the container of my life, dry up, in Jesus' name.

Day 4 (01-09-21)- *The Bible in 70 Days (Day 24-2Kgs 25:12- 1Chron 1:1-11:4)*
Devotional Songs (Pages 4-10)
Praise and Worship
Prayers of Praise and Thanksgiving (Page 13)

85. Evil personality following me about, be separated from me, in Jesus' name.

86. Every power assigned to turn my glory to shame, die, in the name of Jesus.

87. Powers hiding evil materials in my body to torment me, die, in Jesus' name.

88. Battle of the mighty against my destiny, expire, in the name of Jesus.

89. My glory, reject evil command, in the name of Jesus.

90. Any serpentine broom assigned to sweep away good things from my life, catch fire and burn to ashes, in the name of Jesus.

91. All the powers preparing poison for me, drink your poison, in Jesus' name.

92. Every garment of wickedness assigned against my life, catch fire, in the name of Jesus.

93. Every power that says I will not rest will not know peace, in the name of Jesus.

94. Every dark hand waging war against my destiny, die by fire, in Jesus' name.

95. Any mistake attracting suffering to me, be corrected today, in Jesus' name.

96. Every battle of working without reward, scatter by fire, in the name of Jesus.

97. Ancestral curses waiting for the day of my glory to manifest, break, in the name of Jesus.

98. Garment of my ancestors forced upon me, catch fire, in the name of Jesus.

99. Fire of God, locate the strongroom of the wicked elders and recover my virtues for me, in the name of Jesus.

100. Every power, surrounding me in the kingdom of darkness, scatter by fire, in the name of Jesus.

101. My blessings, hear my voice, arise and locate me, in the name of Jesus.

102. Animals of darkness attached to my destiny, die, in the name of Jesus.

103. Anyone using my pictures to steal my virtues, run mad and die, in the name of Jesus.

104. By the blood of Jesus, I refuse to be called a witch in the dream, in the name of Jesus.

105. Every flying witch that wants to use me as a horse, fall down and die, in the name of Jesus.

106. Any bile, blood and palm-oil poured into water to harm my star, backfire and release the glory of my star, in the name of Jesus.

107. Shrine of demons operating against my life and against the lives of my family members, invoke yourself to the grave and die, in the name of Jesus.

108. Any satanic magnet of unexplainable high debt in my life, be rolled off by the blood of Jesus, in the name of Jesus.

109. Witchcraft powers using my sweat and that of my family members against us, lose your power and die, in the name of Jesus.

110. Every witchcraft agent crossing legs and hands against me, collapse and die, in the name of Jesus.

111. Every village masquerade chasing me day and night, catch fire and burn to ashes, in the name of Jesus.

112. Every strange eye from the water, looking at me and the members of my family, go blind now, in the name of Jesus.

Day 5 (02-09-21) - *The Bible in 70 Days (Day 25 - 1 Chronicles 11:5-27:12)*
Devotional Songs (Pages 4-10)
Praise and Worship
Prayers of Praise and Thanksgiving (Page 13)

113. The victory of darkness over my life, scatter by fire, in the name of Jesus.

114. Every satanic rearrangement of my destiny, be readjusted in my favour by the blood of Jesus, in the name of Jesus.

115. Collective family captivity, see me and my family members no more; and swallow your owner, in the name of Jesus.

116. Any walking curse in my life, die, in the name of Jesus.

117. Blood of Jesus, fight on my behalf and release my finances from the hands of witches, in the name of Jesus.

118. Any arrow fired against my glory to slow me down, be destroyed by fire, in the name of Jesus.

119. Any area of my life opened to all kinds of satanic arrows, be closed by fire, in the name of Jesus.

120. Every arrow assigned to settle on my head, backfire, in the name of Jesus.

121. Generational arrow troubling my life, get out of my life, in the name of Jesus.

122. Invisible spirit oppressing me while I am asleep, fire of God, consume it to ashes, in the name of Jesus.

123. Dark arrows fired to my bed to subdue my destiny, die, in the name of Jesus.

124. If I have been suffering under mistargeted arrows of the wicked, Holy Ghost, arise and return the arrows to their senders, in the name of Jesus.

125. Every close enemy firing arrows into my life, your time is up, die, in the name of Jesus.

126. Unsettled spirit troubling the peace of my mind, clear away by fire, in the name of Jesus.

127. Powers using evil bird to slow down my destiny, die, in the name of Jesus.

128. Any wicked animal standing as Goliath in my life, fall and rise no more, in the name of Jesus.

129. Powerful hand of God that delivers from battle, arise and fight for me, in the

name of Jesus.

130. Powers sending animals to destroy me in my dreams, die suddenly, in the name of Jesus.

131. I recover the blessings that I have lost to any evil animal, in Jesus' name.

132. You my enemies, fall on the sword you prepared for me, in Jesus' name.

133. Curse of the Lord, swallow the head of my battle, in the name of Jesus.

134. My Father, let the struggle of the enemies against me be in vain, in the name of Jesus.

135. O God, arise and disgrace my blackmailers, in the name of Jesus.

136. Stubborn powers preventing my battles from dying, die, in Jesus' name.

137. Powers that want me to come to this world in vain, die, in the name of Jesus.

138. Powers deciding how long I will live, run mad, in the name of Jesus.

139. Any long-staying arrow, in my life, die, in the name of Jesus.

140. Arrows that have been pestering anyone in my family, catch fire, in the name of Jesus.

Day 6 (03-09-21) - *The Bible in 70 Days (Day 26-1Chn 27:13-2Chn 1:1- 18:23)*
Devotional Songs (Pages 4-10)
Praise and Worship
Prayers of Praise and Thanksgiving (Page 13)

141. Powers seeking for my glory for demonic fame, die, in the name of Jesus.

142. Powers confronting my destiny with battles, O God, judge them quickly, in the name of Jesus.

143. O Lord, let Your raging fire destroy those dancing to kill me, in Jesus' name.

144. Every problem that will make me live with bad stories for the rest of my life, die, in the name of Jesus.

145. From every battle of 'no escape for you', O God, arise and deliver me quickly, in the name of Jesus.

146. Powers announcing my death while I am still alive, be wasted, in the name of Jesus.

147. Every body of darkness wearing my garment of glory, pull it off and dry up by fire, in the name of Jesus.

PRAYER BATTLE (2)

148. Powers that say they will never give up on me, O Lord, let them be wasted, in the name of Jesus.

149. Every problem that is heavier than my destiny, be terminated now, in the name of Jesus.

150. Demonic serpents sitting on my throne, catch fire and burn to ashes, in the name of Jesus.

151. Anyone using charms to enjoy all that I am supposed to enjoy, by the fire of God, let the charms disappoint him and make him naked, in Jesus' name.

152. Anyone monitoring my prayers and snatching my testimonies from me, run mad and die, in the name of Jesus.

153. Anyone stealing my joy, making me cry and laughing at me, die in disgrace, in the name of Jesus.

154. Any man that has gone to make a covenant with poverty, in my name, so that I can beg from him before I survive, run mad, in the name of Jesus.

155. Lion of darkness, consume those that sent you against me, in Jesus' name.

156. Anyone assigned to steal from me, run mad, in the name of Jesus.

157. Wicked powers hiding to do evil to me, for me to see evil, both you and your evil works shall be consumed by fire, in the name of Jesus.

158. Powers padding me with different gifts of poverty, carry your load and die, in the name of Jesus.

159. Every load of struggle and disappointment, looking like blessings to me, be consumed by fire, in the name of Jesus.

160. Whoever that is born of a woman, that enjoys watching me suffer, run mad, in the name of Jesus.

161. Agent of darkness that has turned himself to cobweb to tie me down, remain as cobweb and be roasted by fire, in the name of Jesus.

162. Every power manipulating the dead to cry against me for no reason, cry to death, in the name of Jesus.

163. Storehouses of tears and battles built up against me, catch fire, in the name of Jesus.

164. Dark battles assigned to destroy my name with shame, die, in Jesus' name.

PRAYER BATTLE (2)

165. Powers assigned to make evil my fate, run mad, in the name of Jesus.

166. Powers using the garment of the dead to kill my destiny, Lion of the tribe of Judah, consume them, in the name of Jesus.

167. Powers assigned to give strangers my glory to use, run mad, in Jesus' name.

168. Every mouth singing the song of 'what a pity' for me shall sing a new song of congratulations for me, in the name of Jesus.

Day 7 (04-09-21) - *The Bible in 70 Days (Day 27 - 2 Chronicles 18:24- 36:16)*
Devotional Songs (Pages 4-10)
Praise and Worship
Prayers of Praise and Thanksgiving (Page 13)

169. Powers giving the power of the dead my garment of greatness to hide, collect it back for me and die, in the name of Jesus.

170. Anointing over my life to be popular for tragedy, dry up by the blood of Jesus, in the name of Jesus.

171. Powers preparing new problems for a new age for me, be suddenly wasted, in the name of Jesus.

172. Every rage of the dead to make me run an errand for them, shut up and die, in the name of Jesus.

173. Strange eyes of the wicked elders, hiding in my head to kill my breakthrough, come out and catch fire, in the name of Jesus.

174. Powers keeping me in an unwanted situation, leave my life alone and die, in the name of Jesus.

175. Iron-like problems disturbing me from moving forward, be terminated now, in the name of Jesus.

176. Strange powers selling me to strange places, blood of Jesus, buy me back, in the name of Jesus.

177. O God, arise and surprise the camp of my enemies with stormy fire, in the name of Jesus.

178. Powers making my days miserable, die suddenly, in the name of Jesus.

179. Sacrifice of darkness putting my life in a situation that I cannot explain, catch fire, in the name of Jesus.

180. What has been making the enemy succeed against my life shall kill him, in the name of Jesus.

181. Every wicked elder that is interested in destroying my life and destiny, die, in the name of Jesus.

182. Wicked elders giving my life to dead spirits to control, O God, arise and rage against them, in the name of Jesus.

183. Wicked personality making a covenant with death in my name, O God, arise and break the covenant and beat him to death, in the name of Jesus.

184. The secret behind the battles against my life, O God, arise, expose it and destroy it, in the name of Jesus.

185. O angel of death, hear the word of the Lord, stop those who want to stop me and destroy those who want to destroy me, in the name of Jesus.

186. Every power that does not want to see me around, your time is up, fall down and die, in the name of Jesus.

187. Every satanic bird crying to make me die, receive the arrow of death, in the name of Jesus.

188. Arrow of serious confusion at the edge of my blessings, scatter by fire, in the name of Jesus.

189. Wicked woman rising up at the edge of my testimony, I press your head down, in the name of Jesus.

190. Bad spirits inspiring me not to move forward, leave my life alone and die, in the name of Jesus.

191. Any demon that has gone to collect my blessings before me, you cannot escape this time. Enough is enough. Give back my blessings to me and die, in the name of Jesus.

192. Battles assigned to grow up with me, die by fire, in the name of Jesus.

193. Wicked elders that have vowed not to give up on me, storm of fire, swallow them, in the name of Jesus.

194. Battles mocking my prayers, scatter by fire, in the name of Jesus.

195. Powers using strange problems to harass me constantly, run mad and die, in the name of Jesus.

PRAYER BATTLE (2)

196. Wicked covenant blocking my efforts from leading to good results, break by fire, in the name of Jesus.

Day 8 (05-09-21) - *The Bible in 70 Days (Day 28 - 2Chr 36:17 - Ne h 1:1-7:33)*
Devotional Songs (Pages 4-10)
Praise and Worship
Prayers of Praise and Thanksgiving (Page 13)

197. Wicked covenant trailing me about, leave my life alone and break by fire, in the name of Jesus.

198. Battles that have vowed to remain with me from birth to death, be terminated now, in the name of Jesus.

199. 'Unless and except battles' frustrating my destiny, die suddenly, in the name of Jesus.

200. Battles making me to age without meaningful achievement to show for it, scatter by fire, in the name of Jesus.

201. Deaf and dumb battles, release my destiny and die, in the name of Jesus.

202. Every demon transferred from my parents to frustrate me, be consumed by fire, in the name of Jesus.

203. Terrible captivity of my father's house, assigned to make my glory a history while I am still alive, thunder of God, scatter it, in the name of Jesus.

204. Unseen evil legs, following me about to scatter my way, be consumed by fire, in the name of Jesus.

205. Powers attacking me and insulting me, O God, beat them to death, in the name of Jesus.

206. Anointing for hatred placed upon me permanently by my enemies, dry up by fire, in the name of Jesus.

207. O God, arise and curse all my secret troubles to expire, in the name of Jesus.

208. Evil marks that have diverted all my blessings from me, O God, wipe them off and restore my blessings, in the name of Jesus.

209. Wicked workers of the wicked elders killing every joy that is my portion, thunder of God, strike them to death, in the name of Jesus.

210. Every power fighting me for refusing to be robbed, destroy yourself, in the name of Jesus.

PRAYER BATTLE (2)

211. Every power fighting me for refusing to be enslaved, die, in Jesus' name.

212. Any arrow of sluggishness at the edge of my breakthroughs, die, in the name of Jesus.

213. Enough is enough. Wherever the source of this arrow of reproach is, I command you to return to the head of the sender by fire, in Jesus' name.

214. Every unrepentant enemy of my progress, fight yourself and die, in the name of Jesus.

215. Mockery and shame, leave my life alone and die, in the name of Jesus.

216. O Lord, shake the kingdom of darkness with thunder and let it regret knowing my name, in the name of Jesus.

217. My mockers shall fall into the hands of destroyers that are stronger than they to waste them, in the name of Jesus.

218. My enemies shall use all the resources they have to buy calamity and tragedy, in the name of Jesus.

219. Defilement of darkness, you shall not swallow my destiny, expire, in the name of Jesus.

220. Every arrow in my life that exposed me to troubles, leave my life alone and die, in the name of Jesus.

221. O God, arise and consume the terror of my enemies, in the name of Jesus.

222. O God, arise and make my enemies food for themselves, in Jesus' name.

223. Fire of deliverance to destroy embargoes, come into my life, in Jesus' name.

224. O God, arise and put my enemies in the disaster they can never escape from, in the name of Jesus.

Day 9 (06-09-21) - *The Bible in 70 Days (Day 29 - Neh 7:34 - Job 1:1-2:6)*
Devotional Songs (Pages 4-10)
Praise and Worship
Prayers of Praise and Thanksgiving (Page 13)

225. The weapons of war possessed by my enemies shall slay them, in the name of Jesus.

226. O God, arise and let the running around of my enemies to destroy me push me to my throne, in the name of Jesus.

227. O God, confuse every confusion assigned against me; and waste every waster assigned against me, in the name of Jesus.

228. The blood that my enemies drank from me shall turn to acid and kill them, in the name of Jesus.

229. The food that my enemies prepared to swallow my destiny will be the food they will eat and die instantly, in the name of Jesus.

230. Every book of remembrance of darkness working against me, catch fire, in the name of Jesus.

231. My breakthrough in the room of the enemy, come out by fire, in the name of Jesus.

232. O Lord, force my enemies to drink the poison they prepared for me, in the name of Jesus.

233. End of the year battles, you shall not locate me or my family, die, in the name of Jesus.

234. O God, arise and tear my enemies to pieces, so that I will celebrate, in the name of Jesus.

235. O God, arise, force my enemies to drink the water of shame and disgrace that they want to feed me with for the rest of this year, in the name of Jesus.

236. Thunder of God, destroy the producer of battle in my life that has vowed to make the rest of this year hell for me, in the name of Jesus.

237. Stubborn voice of darkness that has vowed to oppress me and waste me this year, O God, shut it up forever, in the name of Jesus.

238. Anyone accepting evil mark to destroy me, run mad and die, in Jesus' name.

239. O God, arise and wipe my name from the charge sheet of the wicked elders, in the name of Jesus.

240. Wherever I have been condemned to deadly battle, O God, answer them there by fire and destruction, in the name of Jesus.

241. Undertakers of my destiny from the wicked elders, be buried in your own graves, in the name of Jesus.

242. Father, let every evil word hurting my destiny go back to its sender, in the name of Jesus.

PRAYER BATTLE (2)

243. Thorns of darkness growing on the field of my destiny, clear away and catch fire, in the name of Jesus.

244. O God, arise and break every pot cooking crisis and confusion into my glory, in the name of Jesus.

245. Powers pushing me into the way of killers, wasters, pit makers and gravediggers, be wasted quickly, in the name of Jesus.

246. Every backbiter of darkness around my life, bite the dust forever, in the name of Jesus.

247. Lord, turn the air-conditioners of my tormentors into a burning fire, in the name of Jesus.

248. Demonic policemen sending my helpers away, scatter by fire, in the name of Jesus.

249. Powers assigned to make my reproach a volume of books for the whole world to read, run mad, in the name of Jesus.

250. Arrows of darkness assigned to turn my water to wilderness, backfire, in the name of Jesus.

251. Powers exchanging my health with a strange garment, die, in Jesus' name.

252. Lord of hosts, set Your fire upon the evil pot assigned to drain the blood of my health, in the name of Jesus.

Day 10 (07-09-21) - *The Bible in 70 Days (Day 30 - Job 2:7-20:15)*
Devotional Songs (Pages 4-10)
Praise and Worship
Prayers of Praise and Thanksgiving (Page 13)

253. Satanic expiry date on my health, be destroyed right now, in Jesus' name.

254. Lord, destroy every witchcraft and occult burial done in my name, in the name of Jesus.

255. Wild lions and wolves of the wicked elders seeking my blood, fight yourselves and die, in the name of Jesus.

256. O Lord, blind the eye of every wicked elder cursing my increase, in the name of Jesus.

257. Battle of irregular favour, die, in the name of Jesus.

258. Battles assigned to make me expose myself to shame before I can get favour, die, in the name of Jesus.

259. Bondage builder, I render you jobless and useless in my life, in Jesus' name.

260. Every shadow of darkness the enemy has cast over me to prevent my life from shining, backfire, in the name of Jesus.

261. Every old and wicked garment assigned to pursue every blessing that comes my way, I set you ablaze by fire, in the name of Jesus.

262. Dark powers seeking for my shame shall die for my sake, in Jesus' name.

263. In the name of Jesus, I shall not eat the bread of sorrow; I shall not eat the bread of shame; and I shall not eat the bread of defeat.

264. Load of darkness releasing one sickness or another into my life, be consumed by fire, in the name of Jesus.

265. River of darkness spreading problems in my life, dry up by fire, in the name of Jesus.

266. Every satanic joy over the problem that looks like it has no solution in my life, be disappointed, in the name of Jesus.

267. Unstoppable arrows living in my destiny, fire of God, scatter them now, in the name of Jesus.

268. Lord, let the sun of destruction consume my tormentors, in Jesus' name.

269. Whatever the enemies know about me and they are using to afflict me, thunder of God, destroy their heads, in the name of Jesus.

270. Anyone visiting crossroads to curse me, run mad and die, in Jesus' name.

271. Powers hiding my garment of honour and replacing it with a garment of disgrace, release my garment of honour and die suddenly, in Jesus' name.

272. Powers that have vowed to feed permanently on my sufferings, Lion of the tribe of Judah, arrest them and consume them, in the name of Jesus.

273. Powers punishing my destiny as if I don't know how to pray, run mad and die, in the name of Jesus.

274. Powers making me to suffer and have vowed never to leave me, O God, arise and judge them quickly, in the name of Jesus.

275. Powers that have vowed to make frustration my food, O God, arise and beat

them to death, in the name of Jesus.

276. Powers that say they will make life difficult for me and see how God will save me, O God, let them pay with their blood, in the name of Jesus.

277. Powers planting arrows in me for people to think that I am my own enemy, swallow your arrows and die, in the name of Jesus.

278. Information about me that the enemies are using to afflict me, thunder of God, destroy it, in the name of Jesus.

279. Evil arrows living inside my destiny, fire of God, flush them out now, in the name of Jesus.

280. Lord, let the sun of destruction shine to consume all my tormentors, in the name of Jesus.

SECTION CONFESSIONS

It is written, "If God be for us, who can be against us?" God is with me; I have no reason to fear, in the name of Jesus. I receive the ammunition of angelic guidance and operations in my life right now, in the name of Jesus. The angels have been ordered by God to take charge of me in all my ways and I receive them; they go ahead of me wherever I go and in whatever I do; they go forth and make all the crooked ways straight for me, in the name of Jesus. The angels of God watch over me in the day time and in the night time. They make sure that no evil whatsoever befalls me, in Jesus' name. I send the angels of God to pursue all my enemies and make them like chaff in the wind, in the name of Jesus. I also send a grievous whirlwind to hit them, to destroy them and cast them into the bottomless pit, in the name of Jesus.

In the name of Jesus Christ, the mighty hand of God is upon my life, upholding and protecting me from all who rise up against me, in the name of Jesus. Jesus Christ has made His grace available to me. I ask for the grace and I receive it by faith, in the name of Jesus. I can do and possess all things, through Christ who strengthens me. And my God shall supply all my needs, according to His riches in glory by Christ Jesus. My heart is from now comforted, for the God of suddenly, provision and grace is still on the throne, in the name of Jesus.

SECTION VIGIL

(To be done at night between the hours of 12 midnight and 2 am)

HYMN FOR THE VIGIL (Pages 10-11)

1. Holy Ghost fire, pursue every poison out of my body, in the name of Jesus.
2. Any arrow in my body, currently in the brain, come out by fire, in Jesus' name.
3. My heavens be permanently open by the power in the blood of Jesus.
4. Every miracle blocker, breakthrough blocker, prayer blocker, I am not your candidate, I render your work useless, in the name of Jesus.
5. Blood of Jesus, nullify any evil plan set to work against me, in Jesus' name.
6. Prayer blocker sending incantation to the heavenlies against me, expire, in the name of Jesus.
7. Powers hiding in the storm to steal my testimonies, die, in the name of Jesus.
8. Every evil smoke going to heaven to block the source of my happiness, scatter by fire, in the name of Jesus.
9. O God, arise and consume every evil altar suspending the agenda of heaven for my sake, in the name of Jesus.
10. Powers going from altar to altar to work against my breakthroughs, be exposed by fire and die, in the name of Jesus.
11. Heaven blocker hear the word of the Lord, clear away from the atmosphere of my destiny, in the name of Jesus.
12. Any power that wants to use me to renew its own life, die by fire, in the name of Jesus.
13. Anointing to destroy all the battles assigned against me, fall upon my life, in the name of Jesus.
14. Anointing, authority and power that are enough to settle my case, overshadow my life, in the name of Jesus.
15. Powers hiding me from my showers of blessings, be cut off, in Jesus' name.
16. Power of Herod targeting my plans to prosper, die, in the name of Jesus.
17. Powers assigned to make me see goodness as madness, get out of my life, in the name of Jesus.
18. Spirit of dustbin pursuing good things away from me, get out of my life and die, in the name of Jesus.
19. Any power assigned to collect my gold and replace it with stones, be destroyed, in the name of Jesus.
20. Every hand snatching my benefits away, be roasted by fire, in Jesus' name.
21. Powers using frustration to tie my world, Holy Ghost, pull them down, in the name of Jesus.

SECTION 4 - CONNECTING THE UNLIMITED POWER OF BLOOD

Scripture Reading: Joshua 6
Confession: Job 13:18-19: Behold now, I have ordered my cause; I know that I shall be justified. Who is he that will plead with me? for now, if I hold my tongue, I shall give up the ghost.

Day 1 (08-09-21) - *The Bible in 70 Days (Day 31 -Job 20:16 - 37:16)*
Devotional Songs (Pages 4-10)
Praise and Worship
Prayers of Praise and Thanksgiving (Page 13)

1. Captivity makers keeping me in captivity for me never to taste the blessings attached to my glory, pay with your blood and release me, in Jesus' name.

2. The glory my enemy hid from me so that I can never use it in my lifetime, angel of God, collect it back for me by fire, in the name of Jesus.

3. Every wicked covenant making me to work for my enemies, to feed on my gains, break by fire, in the name of Jesus.

4. Powers marrying me to strange captivity, die, in the name of Jesus.

5. Every problem from the realm of darkness, making me to walk physically and spiritually into cobwebs, be destroyed by fire, in the name of Jesus.

6. O my Strong Tower, shelter me from the stormy blast of my enemies, in the name of Jesus.

7. O treasures hid in the sand, O abundance of the sea, O blessings of the heavens, hear the word of the Lord: gather yourselves together and promote me, in the name of Jesus.

8. Every gap between my minimum blessings and my potential maximum blessings, close up now, in the name of Jesus.

9. Father, turn me into a ball of Holy Ghost fire who cannot be toyed with, in the name of Jesus.

10. Whatever the enemies of my destiny are using to reinforce against me, be consumed by the fire of the Holy Ghost, in the name of Jesus.

11. My glory in the hands of those reinforcing against me, be released by fire, in the name of Jesus.

12. Power that does not want the good things that work for other people to work

for me, die, in the name of Jesus.

13. Bullets of darkness assigned to turn me to a slave, go back to your sender, in the name of Jesus.

14. Powers choosing the date of death and burial for my life, die suddenly, in the name of Jesus.

15. Evil ones hiding in my spirit to celebrate evil, thunder of God, strike them to death, in the name of Jesus.

16. You wicked elders, hear the word of the Lord, pack all your charms away from my destiny, in the name of Jesus.

17. Strange blood upon my life, be eliminated by the blood of Jesus, in the name of Jesus.

18. God of mercy and power, focus on my life, in the name of Jesus.

19. Every satanic power using knife to strangulate my destiny, catch fire, in the name of Jesus.

20. Strangers of darkness attacking and pursuing me with knives, kill yourselves, in the name of Jesus.

21. Wicked powers assigned to use me as a sacrifice on the day of my joy, pay with your own blood, in the name of Jesus.

22. You powers using the face of a familiar person in my family to waste me, fall down and die, in the name of Jesus.

23. Any power that made covenant with the gods about me, be destroyed, in the name of Jesus.

24. I release myself from the bondage of occult friends, in the name of Jesus.

25. My desperate enemy, receive the leprosy of divine judgement, in Jesus' name.

26. Those carrying sacrifices on their heads because of me, run mad and die, in the name of Jesus.

27. I bind every sign of tragedy and sorrow at the edge of my divine blessings, in the name of Jesus.

28. Blood of Jesus, hide me from my enemies today and forever, in Jesus' name.

PRAYER BATTLE (2)

Day 2 (09-09-21) - *The Bible in 70 Days (Day 32 - Job 37:17 Psalms 1:1-22:25)*
Devotional Songs (Pages 4-10)
Praise and Worship
Prayers of Praise and Thanksgiving (Page 13)

29. Whatever form of satanic detour is planned for me and my family, backfire, in the name of Jesus.

30. I come against any kind of sudden disaster lurking in the dark against me, in the name of Jesus.

31. Powers giving me a strange virtue to waste my life, run mad and die, in the name of Jesus.

32. Powers of the wicked elders assigned to make me find myself in trouble in place of celebration, O God, arise and judge them quickly, in Jesus' name.

33. Demonic apprentice using my destiny as a tool for attacks, die suddenly, in the name of Jesus.

34. Powers sending problems to me whenever I want to move forward, die with your load, in the name of Jesus.

35. Any sickness programmed into my body to stop my progress, die, in the name of Jesus.

36. Any power that has locked me up, release me by thunder, in Jesus' name.

37. Every power struggling to close the door of my goodness, be disgraced, in the name of Jesus.

38. Every mark of 'experience no success' placed on my destiny, blood of Jesus, wash it away, in the name of Jesus.

39. Powers terminating every good thing that has been easy for me to get in life, be wasted, in the name of Jesus.

40. Any power preventing people from blessing me, be paralysed, in Jesus' name.

41. Any battle assigned to close the door of my joy, die, in the name of Jesus.

42. Evil mouth spoiling my testimony, catch fire, in the name of Jesus.

43. Any mouth chanting against my testimony, be silenced by fire, in Jesus' name.

44. Lion of the tribe of Judah, destroy all my testimony killers now, in Jesus' name.

45. Testimony killers, I sentence you to compulsory madness, in the name of Jesus.

46. O God of vengeance, visit the enemies of my testimonies with Your anger, in the name of Jesus.

47. Enemies of my multiple testimony, receive divine bullets, in the name of Jesus.

48. O God, arise and let all the enemies of my testimonies be punished by Your anger, in the name of Jesus.

49. Anyone going to any length to use charms against me, run mad and die, in the name of Jesus.

50. Anyone using evil means to steal from me, be destroyed by fire, in the name of Jesus.

51. Every wall of darkness caging me, angel of God, break it now, in Jesus' name.

52. Kingdom of darkness raising up dead battles in my life, thunder of God, scatter it, in the name of Jesus.

53. Wicked powers wasting my life in battle, die, in the name of Jesus.

54. Powers placing battles on my hands and saying that I should keep fighting them, carry your load and die, in the name of Jesus.

55. Powers hissing at me that celebration can never come my way, receive angelic slap, in the name of Jesus.

56. Wicked powers arranging my life to be due for death, arrow of God, kill them, in the name of Jesus.

Day 3 (10-09-21) - *The Bible in 70 Days (Day 33 - Psalms 22:26 - 50:5)*
Devotional Songs (Pages 4-10)
Praise and Worship
Prayers of Praise and Thanksgiving (Page 13)

57. Powers using the wicked agent that is close to me against me, O God, arise and sacrifice him for my comfort, in the name of Jesus.

58. Anointing of darkness backing up strange battles in my life, dry up by fire, in the name of Jesus.

59. Every wicked dance against my destiny, backfire, in the name of Jesus.

60. Every pronouncement of evil to behead me or make me lose my head, die, in the name of Jesus.

61. The convenient day of the enemy over my life and destiny, become the day of

his violent death, in the name of Jesus.

62. O Lord, with blinding speed, destroy my strong enemies and crush all their backups, in the name of Jesus.

63. My Father, destroy every high problem bringing me down, in Jesus' name.

64. O God, arise and turn the fruit that my enemies feed on to the poison of fire, in the name of Jesus.

65. Every power assigned to backstab me, stab yourself, in the name of Jesus.

66. Unrelenting destroyers living in my destiny, leave my life alone and die in frustration, in the name of Jesus..

67. O grave, swallow every suppression and repression of the enemy assigned to frustrate me, in the name of Jesus.

68. Grave diggers and their agents, fall into the graves you prepared for me, in the name of Jesus.

69. Wicked powers sending evil shadows to obstruct and void my prayers, be consumed by the fire of God, in the name of Jesus.

70. Kidnappers of darkness that have taken hold of my glory, O God, arise and tear them to pieces, in the name of Jesus.

71. Strange battles assigned to return me into bondage, die, in the name of Jesus.

72. Every veil of the enemy covering the hearts of my helpers against me, I tear you off by fire, in the name of Jesus.

73. Coat of death, satanically sewn to cause my death, I reject you. Go back to your sender, in the name of Jesus.

74. Every power creating problems and strange situations to mess up my life, Rock of Ages, grind it to powder, in the name of Jesus.

75. Powers that are angry with me and want to destroy me for no reason, run mad and die, in the name of Jesus.

76. O God, arise and do not let Your anger against the wicked go down, until their wickedness terminates them, in the name of Jesus.

77. Powers that have vowed to make me suffer for doing the right thing, be destroyed suddenly, in the name of Jesus.

78. Wicked elders working hard to make me run mad with my potential, O God,

arise and waste them in Your anger, in the name of Jesus.

79. Sword of darkness assigned to cut off my horn of progress, catch fire, in the name of Jesus.

80. Every destiny and glory grabber riding on my horse of destiny, somersault and die, in the name of Jesus.

81. Every demonic tree standing as a sign of no solution to impossible situations in my life, sword of God, cut it down, in the name of Jesus.

82. Powers dragging my destiny on the dark road, release my destiny and die, in the name of Jesus.

83. Evil men testifying against me before the wicked elders to put my destiny into trouble, be disappointed, in the name of Jesus.

84. Powers planning to make me a victim of conspiracy to multiply my battle, be terminated, in the name of Jesus.

Day 4 (11-09-21) - *The Bible in 70 Days (Day 34 - Psalms 50:6 - 78:4)*
Devotional Songs (Pages 4-10)
Praise and Worship
Prayers of Praise and Thanksgiving (Page 13)

85. Lustful judges of darkness seeking my death, run mad and die, in Jesus' name.

86. Every secret conspiracy assigned to make me live in reproach and tears, scatter by fire, in the name of Jesus.

87. Powers assigned to swallow my glory when I am about to receive mercy, receive the arrow of death, in the name of Jesus.

88. Battles assigned to divert my lifetime benefit, scatter by fire, in Jesus' name.

89. Every voice of battle rejecting my blessings, I silence you by fire, in the name of Jesus.

90. Battles making me to suffer last minute disappointment, expire by fire, in the name of Jesus.

91. Any witchcraft voice attacking my endorsement for great things, expire by fire, in the name of Jesus.

92. Any strange voice that always appears whenever I am to be blessed, expire now, in the name of Jesus.

PRAYER BATTLE (2)

93. Any contrary voice that sounds louder when I am to be remembered for something great, be silenced, in the name of Jesus.

94. Dark powers assigned to make me a bad story while I am still alive, O God, arise and judge them quickly, in the name of Jesus.

95. Sudden problems, unexpected problems, assigned to mock me, scatter by fire, in the name of Jesus.

96. Terrible storm of darkness assigned to flood me and my family with troubles, backfire, in the name of Jesus.

97. Every troublesome problem in my life, giving me a bad name, die, in the name of Jesus.

98. Every power that says my waiting on God will end in nakedness, receive the slap of death, in the name of Jesus.

99. Strange battles bringing sweat and struggle, lack, non-achievement and backwardness into my life, scatter by fire, in the name of Jesus.

100. Strange battles messing me up, mocking my destiny, frustrating my efforts, scatter by fire, in the name of Jesus.

101. Strange battles arising from unknown covenants, affecting my progress in life, scatter by fire, in the name of Jesus.

102. Battles of strange tongue raging against my lifting and success, catch fire, in the name of Jesus.

103. Battles of mistakes and errors programmed to affect my success in life, scatter by fire, in the name of Jesus.

104. Self battles, battles of negative characters, affecting my progress, scatter by fire, in the name of Jesus.

105. Battles of failure at the edge of success, growing along with my destiny, be terminated by fire, in the name of Jesus.

106. Battles assigned to catch up with me and scatter my progress at a particular age, die, in the name of Jesus.

107. Any strange battle standing like a wall of Jericho between me and my next breakthrough, collapse, in the name of Jesus.

108. Any battle in my life asking for my God, bow to the name of Jesus, in the

PRAYER BATTLE (2)

name of Jesus.

109. Destiny crippling battles, leave my life alone and die, in the name of Jesus.

110. Garment of the wicked elders carrying my name, keeping me too long in my problems, catch fire, in the name of Jesus.

111. Powers honouring the dead against me, receive the judgement of death, in the name of Jesus.

112. Every king of witchcraft putting my life under threat, receive the arrow of destruction, in the name of Jesus.

Day 5 (12-09-21) - *The Bible in 70 Days (Day 35 - Psalms 78:5 - 103:12)*
Devotional Songs (Pages 4-10)
Praise and Worship
Prayers of Praise and Thanksgiving (Page 13)

113. Powers that have vowed to kill me before my life tastes success, destroy yourselves mercilessly, in the name of Jesus.

114. Evil hands of darkness killing God's best for me, catch fire, in Jesus' name.

115. Powers transferring their problems to my life, carry your load and die, in the name of Jesus.

116. Thou kingdom of darkness deciding on when I should cry and when I should laugh, scatter by thunder, in the name of Jesus.

117. Powers signing me up for short life in the kingdom of darkness, die suddenly, in the name of Jesus.

118. You, demon on assignment to follow me everywhere I go and to frustrate me, be consumed by fire, in the name of Jesus.

119. Powers that tied my life to a demonic tree, leave my life alone and die, in the name of Jesus.

120. Wicked elders assigned to wash my head with the blood of an animal, run mad and die, in the name of Jesus.

121. Every spirit of poverty and suffering that the enemy added to my life, die by fire, in the name of Jesus.

122. Every scorpion planted in my life to eat the content of my destiny, die, in the name of Jesus.

123. Strangers that can predict my life and my destiny, you are liars, die, in the name of Jesus.

124. Pursuing powers from the grave, I bury you now, in the name of Jesus.

125. My star buried in the belly of the wicked elders, come out by fire, in the name of Jesus.

126. Lord, let the stones that the wicked ones prepared against me become bullets of fire and destroy them, in the name of Jesus.

127. Dark powers assigned to make my problem heavier than my glory, die, in the name of Jesus.

128. Every problem in my life that is bigger than my solution, O God, arise and swallow them with Your fire, in the name of Jesus.

129. Problem without solution assigned to swallow me, die, in the name of Jesus.

130. Every problem in my life that does not want to bow to my prayers, die, in the name of Jesus.

131. Problems that disgrace men openly, you shall not locate me, expire, in the name of Jesus.

132. Any witch in league with strange people to multiply my problems, thunder of God, destroy her, in the name of Jesus.

133. You, pillar of my problem, crumble by fire, in the name of Jesus.

134. Powers secretly rejoicing at my problems, hand of God, transfer the problems to their heads, in the name of Jesus.

135. Every problem in my life that is too rigid to be overcome, be voided by the blood of Jesus, in the name of Jesus.

136. Wicked hands covering my eyes from seeing solutions to my problems, catch fire, in the name of Jesus.

137. Evil altar assigned to swallow the gains of my sweats, catch fire, in the name of Jesus.

138. O God, arise and let the expectations of the wicked elders against me turn to dust, in the name of Jesus.

139. Powers waiting to see me suffer shame, run mad, in the name of Jesus.

140. Demonic powers eating sacrifices to conclude their assignments against me,

thunder of God, strike them to death, in the name of Jesus.

Day 6 (13-09-21) - *The Bible in 70 Days (Day 36 - Psalms 103:13 - 119:107)*
Devotional Songs (Pages 4-10)
Praise and Worship
Prayers of Praise and Thanksgiving (Page 13)

141. My best picture used against me in the coven of witchcraft, become a sword of death and destroy them, in the name of Jesus.

142. Battles making me despair to accept that I will never make it again, die, in the name of Jesus.

143. Powers assigned to turn my life to a strange case, O God, arise and judge them quickly, in the name of Jesus.

144. Powers assigned to make my destiny get used to frustration, die, in the name of Jesus.

145. Wicked animals, hear the word of the Lord, come out of my destiny by fire, in the name of Jesus.

146. O God, arise and let Your shadow arise against all my enemies, in the name of Jesus.

147. O God, arise and let Your shadow deliver me from the shadow of death, in the name of Jesus.

148. Blood of Jesus, remove my name from the list of my enemy, in Jesus' name.

149. Powers exposing me to unending battles, die, in the name of Jesus.

150. Powers of darkness assigned to scatter my great expectations, run mad and die, in the name of Jesus.

151. Deep battles that cannot be explained, lose your power over my life and die, in the name of Jesus.

152. Strange problems that are glued to my glory, blood of Jesus, terminate them now, in the name of Jesus.

153. Powers assigned to use me as a scape goat in my family, receive the judgement of death, in the name of Jesus.

154. Dark powers introducing wrong people to me to destroy me, O God, expose and disgrace them, in the name of Jesus.

PRAYER BATTLE (2)

155. Demonic powers tying my hands from producing good results, fire of God, consume them, in the name of Jesus.

156. Wicked elders using me to achieve demonic purpose, thunder of God, destroy them now, in the name of Jesus.

157. Satanic mask causing evil label in my life, catch fire, in the name of Jesus.

158. Every stubborn herbalist working on my case, drink your own blood, in the name of Jesus.

159. Any power within me, assigned to convert me to a living dead, die, in the name of Jesus.

160. Every battle that has stolen my destiny, be terminated now, in Jesus' name.

161. O Lord, take me to where the crown on my head will speak, in Jesus' name.

162. Every power that says I will die in hardship, run mad, in the name of Jesus.

163. Every hand of bitterness, depart from my life, in the name of Jesus.

164. Anything in my life that the power of captivity is using against me, come out by fire, in the name of Jesus.

165. Battle of financial nakedness, leave my life alone and die, in Jesus' name.

166. Powers pursuing my virtues from me, die, in the name of Jesus.

167. My destiny that has been sacrificed to idols, blood of Jesus, bring it back to me, in the name of Jesus.

168. Powers claiming my head for a stranger, receive the arrow of death and die, in the name of Jesus.

Day 7 (14-09-21) - *The Bible in 70 Days (Day 37 - Psl 119:108 - Prov 1:1-2:16)*
Devotional Songs (Pages 4-10)
Praise and Worship
Prayers of Praise and Thanksgiving (Page 13)

169. Powers that have vowed that I will always face strange troubles, die, in the name of Jesus.

170. Arrow of cursed sickness assigned to kill me, backfire, in the name of Jesus.

171. Demonic presence irritating my angel of blessings, disappear by fire, in the name of Jesus.

172. Powers trapping my life with repeated battles, die, in the name of Jesus.

173. Every power that wants to see my corpse in disgrace, Lion of the tribe of Judah, tear it to pieces, in the name of Jesus.

174. Every strange figure sent to me to flog me to death, go back to your sender, in the name of Jesus.

175. O God, arise and put my enemies to the shame that they can never escape from, in the name of Jesus.

176. Destructive fire of God, answer every expectation of the wicked against me, in the name of Jesus.

177. Powers using the wind as a weapon to locate and afflict me, thunder of God, strike them to death, in the name of Jesus.

178. Agents of darkness that have collected evil load to use against me, die with your load, in the name of Jesus.

179. Powers assigned to make me commit errors that will disgrace me, die, in the name of Jesus.

180. Battles overfeeding me with sorrows, be terminated now, in Jesus' name.

181. Arrows of darkness assigned to make me tear my own garment of honour, backfire, in the name of Jesus.

182. The glory that my family never used, and that was consumed by wicked powers, be vomited, in the name of Jesus.

183. Finished work of darkness assigned to announce me for tragedy, scatter by fire, in the name of Jesus.

184. I shall not be celebrated for destruction by the power of darkness, in the name of Jesus.

185. Powers that say I will never leave the down position, you are liars, die, in the name of Jesus.

186. Powers mocking my pains, be disappointed by fire, in the name of Jesus.

187. Instruments of darkness hiding in me to block my rising, come out and die, in the name of Jesus.

188. Powers preparing sad news for me to kill my celebration, run mad and die, in the name of Jesus.

189. Powers cursing me to count papers instead of money, receive the arrow of

death, in the name of Jesus.

190. Powers carrying strange sacrifice to make me disgrace myself, run mad with your sacrifice, in the name of Jesus.

191. Strange fingers scattering what gives me joy, catch fire, in Jesus' name.

192. By the power in the blood of Jesus, I refuse to be my own battle, in the name of Jesus.

193. Strange celebration assigned to increase my tears, thunder of God, scatter it now, in the name of Jesus.

194. Envious powers working hard to see my nakedness, be disappointed by fire, in the name of Jesus.

195. Strange rugs covering the land of my destiny, catch fire, in Jesus' name.

196. Powers using strange rugs to steal my virtues, run mad, in Jesus' name.

Day 8 (15-09-21) - *The Bible in 70 Days (Day 38 - Proverbs 2:17-17:20)*
Devotional Songs (Pages 4-10)
Praise and Worship
Prayers of Praise and Thanksgiving (Page 13)

197. My star hidden inside the wall of darkness, come out and shine, in the name of Jesus.

198. Hands of disgrace rubbing my star, catch fire, in the name of Jesus.

199. Powers that want to use battle to make me a battle to someone else, die, in the name of Jesus.

200. Powers planning for my flesh and blood to be accepted by witchcraft, be wasted in your own blood, in the name of Jesus.

201. Powers that want people to see me as a mad person, run mad and die, in the name of Jesus.

202. Powers putting my destiny in trouble, die, in the name of Jesus.

203. Powers driving the car of my destiny to crush it, die, in the name of Jesus.

204. Arrows pushing me to walk in places that will bring trouble to my life, come out and die, in the name of Jesus.

205. Arrows chasing out my glory from my life, catch fire, in the name of Jesus.

206. Powers on assignment to bathe me with fresh battles, O God, arise and judge them quickly, in the name of Jesus.

207. Covenant trees of darkness in my destiny, catch fire, in the name of Jesus.

PRAYER BATTLE (2)

208. Powers planning to kill me and benefit from my death, be suddenly wasted, in the name of Jesus.

209. Every force chasing away my helpers, be paralysed, in the name of Jesus.

210. O God, arise and let Your water flood the desert of my life, in Jesus' name.

211. Strange spirits appearing in form of masquerades to threaten my life, O God, arise and tear them to pieces, in the name of Jesus.

212. Demonic bullets hiding in my destiny, lose your power over my life, in the name of Jesus.

213. Power of the graveyard working to keep me in detention of darkness, die, in the name of Jesus.

214. O God, arise and crush the forces that have taken over my celebration, in the name of Jesus.

215. Powers selling my virtues to strangers, run mad, in the name of Jesus.

216. Sword of God, terminate the flesh of darkness hovering around to disgrace me, in the name of Jesus.

217. Powers borrowing my image for evil, receive the arrow of death, in the name of Jesus.

218. Ugly situations embarrassing my existence, die, in the name of Jesus.

219. Powers controlling my life to live by their charms, be exposed and be disappointed, in the name of Jesus.

220. Thunder of God, answer the wicked elders invoking me to appear in their wicked mirrors, in the name of Jesus.

221. Evil waters assigned to swallow me, dry up, in the name of Jesus.

222. When the old dragon roars at me, thunder of God, strike against him, in the name of Jesus.

223. My virtues in the land of the dead, arise and locate me by fire, in the name of Jesus.

224. O God, arise and let Your hand of power take me out of the maze of confusion to which the wicked ones tied me, in the name of Jesus.

Day 9 (16-09-21) - *The Bible in 70 Days (Day 39 - Prov 17:21- Eccl 1:1-2:4)*

Devotional Songs (Pages 4-10)

Praise and Worship

Prayers of Praise and Thanksgiving (Page 13)

225. Thunder of God, arise and scatter every satanic army warring against my destiny, in the name of Jesus.

226. Powers monitoring my life to report me to my enemies, run mad and die, in the name of Jesus.

227. Altar of perpetual destruction set up against me, be destroyed by the earthquake of the Almighty, in the name of Jesus.

228. O God, arise and let my stubborn problems expire, in the name of Jesus.

229. Power of God, take me away from the valley of tribulation by fire, in the name of Jesus.

230. Evil messages coded into my destiny, be wiped off by the blood of Jesus, in the name of Jesus.

231. Any power using my photograph to manipulate my life, receive angelic slap now, in the name of Jesus.

232. Every deadly incantation used to mention my name at night, thunder of God, answer it, in the name of Jesus.

233. O Lord, let sudden destruction break forth upon my enemies, in the name of Jesus.

234. Thou Lazarus of my destiny detained in the waters, hear the word of the Lord, come out and locate me, in the name of Jesus.

235. Every voice in the waters crying for my battle to be strong, be silenced by fire, in the name of Jesus.

236. Charismatic witchcraft organising evil party against my life, run mad and die, in the name of Jesus.

237. O God, arise and reward every satanic spy in my destiny with madness, in the name of Jesus.

238. Evil twins assigned to destroy my life with shame, receive the judgement of fire, in the name of Jesus.

239. Every satanic rope binding me with evil twins, break and catch fire, in the name of Jesus.

240. Powers making use of my mouth to curse others in the dream and in the physical, O God, arise, expose and disgrace them, in the name of Jesus.

241. Arrows from the dark places of the earth, release me and let me go, in the name of Jesus.

242. Powers planning tribulations for me and my family, O God, arise and disappoint them, in the name of Jesus.

243. Every satanic fortress detaining my blessings, receive the earthquake of the Lord and collapse from your foundation, in the name of Jesus.

244. Lord, let every hidden siege of the enemy in my dreams be scattered by the thunder of Your fire, in the name of Jesus.

245. Wicked elders cursing me, receive the slap of death, in the name of Jesus.

246. Weapon of death hired against me, return to the body of your sender, in the name of Jesus.

247. Occult tongue speaking against me, wither and dry up, in the name of Jesus.

248. Wicked powers making dangerous sacrifice in my name, sleep and never wake up, in the name of Jesus.

249. Evil load from the grave, go back to your sender, in the name of Jesus.

250. Evil load of darkness containing my name, be consumed by fire, in the name of Jesus.

251. Whoever has handed me over to wicked elders for deadly battles, O Lord, waste him without mercy, in the name of Jesus.

252. Demonic city where evil is manufactured against me, I set you ablaze, in the name of Jesus.

Day 10 (17-09-21) - *The Bible in 70 Days (Day 40 - Eccl 2:5 - Isa 1:1- 6:12)*
Devotional Songs (Pages 4-10)
Praise and Worship
Prayers of Praise and Thanksgiving (Page 13)

253. I wash my head with the blood of Jesus to receive the crown of glory, in the name of Jesus.

254. O horn of salvation, save me from the wrath of my adversaries, in the name of Jesus.

255. By the power that lifted up the beggar from the dunghill, O God, arise and promote me to the palace of my destiny, in the name of Jesus.

256. By the power that catapulted the poor from the dust, O God, arise and catapult me into abundance, in the name of Jesus.

257. I shake off the dust of poverty from my life, by the power in the blood of

Jesus, in the name of Jesus.

258. Poverty ravaging my family and my destiny, I shake you into unquenchable fire, in the name of Jesus.

259. You my treasures buried deep in the dust, hear the voice of the Lord, come forth and resurrect my glorious destiny by fire, in the name of Jesus.

260. Horns of wickedness tormenting me in the dream, collide with the Rock of Ages and break into pieces by fire, in the name of Jesus.

261. Every demonic power assigned to mock and ridicule my destiny, be disgraced by fire, in the name of Jesus.

262. Every power hired to humiliate and drag me to begging for bread, be wasted, in the name of Jesus.

263. King of glory, catapult my inheritance to the throne of glory, in Jesus' name.

264. I receive power from on high to catapult my life to the palace of my prosperity, in the name of Jesus.

265. Dust of poverty that has settled on my life, I blow you off by the wind of the Holy Ghost, in the name of Jesus.

266. Poverty and hopelessness of the dunghill, release me now, in Jesus' name.

267. My glory, my glory, my glory, 'What are you doing in the refuse dump?' Arise, locate me and catapult me to the throne of glory, in the name of Jesus.

268. Thou throne of God, overthrow the cubicle of shame in my life, in the name of Jesus.

269. Every altar of trouble given to me as a gift, be consumed by fire, in the name of Jesus.

270. Altar from the pit of hell killing my destiny, catch fire, in the name of Jesus.

271. Stubborn battles that have vowed not to leave me, die, in the name of Jesus.

272. Anyone planning my death shall be exposed and be disgraced, in the name of Jesus.

273. Anyone sent on a mission to destroy my life, be disappointed, in the name of Jesus.

274. Every wicked move assigned to trap me, scatter by fire, in the name of Jesus.

275. Powers disguising to be my helpers to know my secrets and increase my battles, run mad and die, in the name of Jesus.

276. Wicked elders looking for my permission to deal with me, be terminated, in the name of Jesus.

277. Powers provoking me to offend them so that they can attack me, be

disappointed, in the name of Jesus.

278. Powers bringing me down and saying: 'I will never go up in their lifetime', die, in the name of Jesus.

279. O God, arise and remove my name from the negotiation list of the wicked elders, in the name of Jesus.

280. Every satanic joy over any problem that I have, be disappointed, in the name of Jesus.

SECTION CONFESSION

I trample under my feet, every serpent of treachery, evil reports, accusations, machinations and criticisms, in the name of Jesus. In the time of trouble, the Lord my God and my Father shall hide me in His pavilion; in the secret place of His tabernacle shall He hide me. With an overrunning flood, will the Lord make an utter end of my enemy's habitation, in the name of Jesus. The Lord has sent the fear and the dread of me upon all my enemies, that the report or information of me shall cause them to fear, tremble and be in anguish, in the name of Jesus. I am of good cheer, and I believe in the sanctity and infallibility of God's word, in the name of Jesus. According to this time, it shall be said of me and my family, what God has done, in the name of Jesus. I, therefore, command all enemy troops arrayed against me to scatter, as I call down the thunder fire of God upon them, in the name of Jesus.

May the Lord God to whom vengeance belongs pelt their rank, files and strongholds with His stones of fire, in the name of Jesus. I raise a dangerous high standard of the flood of the blood of Jesus against their re-enforcement, and I command all the encamped and advancing enemy troops to be roasted by fire, in the name of Jesus. I possess the gate of my enemies and with the blood of Jesus, I render their habitation desolate, in the mighty name of Jesus Christ.

SECTION VIGIL
(TO BE DONE AT NIGHT BETWEEN THE HOURS OF 12 MIDNIGHT AND 2 AM)
HYMN FOR THE VIGIL (Pages 10-11)

1. Every gap between my minimum blessing and my potential maximum blessing, close, in the name of Jesus.

2. Father, turn me into a ball of Holy Ghost fire that cannot be reinforced against, in the name of Jesus.

3. Whatever the enemies might have been using to reinforce against me, be

consumed by the fire of the Holy Ghost, in the name of Jesus.

4. My glory in the hand of those reinforcing against me, be released, in the name of Jesus.

5. Powers that do not want the good things that work for others to work for me, die, in the name of Jesus.

6. Bullets of darkness assigned to turn me into a slave, go back to the sender, in the name of Jesus.

7. Powers choosing the date of death and burial for my life, die suddenly, in the name of Jesus.

8. Evil ones hiding to celebrate evil against me, thunder of God, strike them to death, in the name of Jesus.

9. You wicked elders, hear the word of the Lord, pack your sorceries away from my destiny, in the name of Jesus.

10. Every strange blood upon my life, be cancelled by the blood of Jesus, in the name of Jesus.

11. God of mercy and power, focus on my life, in the name of Jesus.

12. Every satanic power using the evil night to strangulate my destiny, catch fire, in the name of Jesus.

13. Every stranger of darkness attacking and pursuing me with a knife, kill yourself, in the name of Jesus.

14. Wicked power assigned to use me as a sacrifice on the day of my joy, pay with your blood, in the name of Jesus.

15. Powers using the face of a familiar person in my family to waste my life, fall down and die, in the name of Jesus.

16. Any power that has made any covenant with any idol against me, be destroyed, in the name of Jesus.

17. I release myself from the company of occult friends, in the name of Jesus.

18. My desperate enemy, receive the leprosy of divine judgement, in Jesus' name.

19. Anyone carrying sacrifices to waste my life, be wasted, in the name of Jesus.

20. I bind every sign of tragedy and sorrow at the end of my divine blessing, in the name of Jesus.

21. Blood of Jesus, hide me from secret enemies today and forever, in the name of Jesus.

SECTION 5 - CONNECTING THE BLOOD OF JESUS

Scripture Reading: Exodus 12

Confession: Revelation 12:11 And they overcame him by the blood of the Lamb, and by the word of their testimony; and they loved not their lives unto the death.

Day 1(18-09-21) - *The Bible in 70 Days (Day 41 - Isaiah 6:13-30:8)*

Devotional Songs (Pages 4-10)

Praise and Worship

Prayers of Praise and Thanksgiving (Page 13)

1. O Lord, give me the shoes of iron and brass to scatter the heads of my enemies, in the name of Jesus.

2. Every carefully concealed trap set up against my life, turn around and capture your owner, in the name of Jesus.

3. Any power accepting evil position because of me, perish suddenly by fire, in the name of Jesus.

4. Every power sending strange fire into my life, be consumed by the fire of God, in the name of Jesus.

5. O Lord, let Your angels begin to blow the trumpet of war against my enemies, in the name of Jesus.

6. Wicked elders placing other people's evil load on me, carry the load and die suddenly, in the name of Jesus.

7. Every throne of the wicked spirit deciding on my case, scatter and burn to ashes, in the name of Jesus.

8. Food of sorrow and weeping prepared for me, catch fire, in the name of Jesus.

9. Arrows killing Godly virtues in my life, come out and die, in the name of Jesus.

10. Marine poison in my destiny, blood of Jesus, wash it away, in Jesus' name.

11. Battles assigned to kill me slowly, die, in the name of Jesus.

12. Every food that will kill my destiny, be consumed by fire, in the name of Jesus.

13. Powers assigned to use food to cover my glory, enough is enough, be terminated now, in the name of Jesus.

PRAYER BATTLE (2)

14. Strangers preparing me for long term poverty, receive the arrow of death, in the name of Jesus.

15. Powers using my body for strange and evil works, O Lord, tear them to pieces, in the name of Jesus.

16. My close enemies stealing my virtues, be exposed and be disgraced, in the name of Jesus.

17. O God, arise and separate me from the bondage of slavery and shame in which the wicked ones have held me, in the name of Jesus.

18. Every graveyard food prepared for me, catch fire, in the name of Jesus.

19. Powers hiding my destiny in the grave, lose your power over me, in the name of Jesus.

20. Wicked elders assigned to confine me in the grave, be wasted, in Jesus' name.

21. Powers sending odour from the burial ground against my glory, run mad, in the name of Jesus.

22. Handshake with the spirit of death, be aborted by fire, in the name of Jesus.

23. O God, arise and turn the coven of the wicked elders to their burial ground, in the name of Jesus.

24. My sleeping glory, arise and meet up with your destiny, in the name of Jesus.

25. I destroy the eyes and the body of the wicked elders working against me, in the name of Jesus.

26. You, my wicked enemies, leave me alone and kill yourselves, in Jesus' name.

27. Powers giving me the problems that do not belong to me, run mad and die, in the name of Jesus.

28. Every power crawling around my destiny, be consumed by fire, in Jesus' name.

Day 2 (19-09-21) - *Reading the Bible in 70 Days (Day 42- Isaiah 30:9 - 50:7)*

Devotional Songs (Pages 4-10)

Praise and Worship

Prayers of Praise and Thanksgiving (Page 13)

29. O God, cause my enemies to cry without help for them, in the name of Jesus.

30. O God, arise, let not my glory feed my enemies, in the name of Jesus.

31. O God, arise and fight my battle in the day and at night, in the name of Jesus.

32. My Father, if my glory has decayed, been damaged or is smelling in the prison where it was kept, O God, arise and restore it perfectly, in the name of Jesus.

33. Battles assigned to keep me in a sorry state, die, in the name of Jesus.

34. Powers assigned to turn the source of my happiness to dust, receive the judgement of death, in the name of Jesus.

35. I refuse to feed my battles, by the power in the blood of Jesus, in Jesus' name.

36. Powers using my problems to compose a negative song for me, sword of God, destroy them, in the name of Jesus.

37. O God, arise and prove to my enemies that my problems can be over, in the name of Jesus.

38. Acid of God, drench the body of all my enemies, in the name of Jesus.

39. Any power hissing at me because of my problems, O God, arise and disappoint him, in the name of Jesus.

40. Any problem that is sharing part of my destiny, lose your hold over my life, in the name of Jesus.

41. Battles that have given me a pitiful name, be terminated now, in Jesus' name.

42. Every strange voice telling me that nothing can be done about my situation, be silenced forever by fire, in the name of Jesus.

43. Handkerchief of slavery covering my glory, catch fire, in the name of Jesus.

44. Every negative anointing of satanic prophet upon my glory, backfire, in the name of Jesus.

45. Dangerous friends reporting my progress to a witch doctor, burn to death, in the name of Jesus.

46. Any bewitched wrapper, given to my mother, that is tormenting my glory, catch fire, in the name of Jesus.

47. Strange words of the wicked promoting captivity in my life, backfire, in the name of Jesus.

48. Powers that are angry with my life, destroy yourselves, in the name of Jesus.

49. Dark powers using a black pot to control my life, burn with your pot, in the name of Jesus.

50. Strange things buried in the ground because of me, swallow my enemies, in

the name of Jesus.

51. Battles attracting strange people to me, expire, in the name of Jesus.

52. Witchcraft ring given to me as a gift, catch fire, in the name of Jesus.

53. Any strange money that I have spent and that has opened the gate of poverty in my life, blood of Jesus, nullify it now, in the name of Jesus.

54. Holy Ghost fire, dry up the anointing of demonic prophet on my head, in the name of Jesus.

55. Thou strange river in my village, holding the larger part of my glory, release it and dry up by fire, in the name of Jesus.

56. Every strange bullet of the wicked, aimed at me by ancestral powers, catch fire, in the name of Jesus.

Day 3 (20-09-21) - *The Bible in 70 Days (Day 43 - Isa 50:8 - Jer 1:1-6:24)*
Devotional Songs (Pages 4-10)
Praise and Worship
Prayers of Praise and Thanksgiving (Page 13)

57. Strange marks exposing me to trouble, expire by fire, in the name of Jesus.

58. Strange altar of the wicked vomiting strange curses upon my life, backfire, in the name of Jesus.

59. Charm of failure and sickness, buried in the ground for me to step on, catch your owner, in the name of Jesus.

60. Power that wants me to disappear when my star appears, die, in Jesus' name.

61. Powers waiting for me to see my testimony before they strike me with sudden death, be wasted by fire, in the name of Jesus.

62. Powers disqualifying me from long life, die, in the name of Jesus.

63. Powers that want me to serve God in rags, run mad and die, in Jesus' name.

64. Powers pushing me into trouble whenever I am preparing to celebrate, O God, arise and expose and disappoint them, in the name of Jesus.

65. Powers drinking blood to make me naked, die a hot death, in Jesus' name.

66. Powers assigned to make me struggle and spend money on sicknesses, thunder of God, strike them to death, in the name of Jesus.

67. Arrow of blockage blocking every good thing that comes my way, scatter by

fire, in the name of Jesus.

68. Wicked powers assigned to give me problems that have no solution, you are too small, die, in the name of Jesus.

69. Wicked elders cursing my glory to fail me, receive angelic slap, in Jesus' name.

70. Battles assigned to make sorrow the result of my labour, be terminated now, in the name of Jesus.

71. Glory-eating demons assigned to consume my glory, fire of God, consume them, in the name of Jesus.

72. Wicked personality paying herbalists to steal my glory and make me empty, run mad and die, in the name of Jesus.

73. My enemies shall eat every one of the words they spoke against me, in the name of Jesus.

74. O God, arise, take me away from the crowd and make me special, in the name of Jesus.

75. O God, arise and let my name open great doors for me, in the name of Jesus.

76. Poison of death flowing in my destiny, dry up by fire, in the name of Jesus.

77. O God, arise and raise enemies against my enemies for my sake, in the name of Jesus.

78. Anyone eating concoction to waste me shall eat poison and die, in the name of Jesus.

79. Battles assigned to turn my salt to sand, die, in the name of Jesus.

80. Powers assigned to scatter my load of joy, run mad, in the name of Jesus.

81. Wicked personality looking for me with violent death, receive the sword of destruction, in the name of Jesus.

82. My destiny, jump out of the moving vehicle of death and destruction, in the name of Jesus.

83. Powers waiting to hear bad news about me, O God, kill them with my great testimony, in the name of Jesus.

84. Ancestral garments covering my star, catch fire, in the name of Jesus.

PRAYER BATTLE (2)

Day 4 (21-09-21) - *The Bible in 70 Days (Day 44-Jeremiah 6:25-25:23)*

Devotional Songs (Pages 4-10)

Praise and Worship

Prayers of Praise and Thanksgiving (Page 13)

85. Satanic negotiation against my glory, scatter by fire, in the name of Jesus.

86. I reject every report of fear sent to me , in the name of Jesus.

87. You, satanic fear, lose your power over my life , in the name of Jesus.

88. The evil everyone dreads will not locate me and my family, in Jesus' name.

89. Fire of destruction, fall upon the head of every demon working against my destiny, in the name of Jesus.

90. Demonic powers arresting my future, lose your power over me and die, in the name of Jesus.

91. Sword of destruction, locate the head of my enemies, in the name of Jesus.

92. Every spiritual horseman riding away with my miracle, fall down and die, in the name of Jesus.

93. Satanic smoke assigned to blow my blessings away, scatter by fire, in the name of Jesus.

94. Powers setting up a sleeping gas against my destiny, die, in the name of Jesus.

95. Any herbalist using my cloth to cause problem for me, die, in Jesus' name.

96. Anyone using the history of my problems against me shall witness my testimony, in the name of Jesus.

97. Any problem assigned to add problem to my destiny, die, in the name of Jesus.

98. Any problem that has covenant with the night on my life, expire, in the name of Jesus.

99. Satanic pot cooking concoction to poison me, break and scatter by fire, in the name of Jesus.

100. Every power of fatigue wearing me down, be swept away by fire, in the name of Jesus.

101. Every smoke of darkness sending battles into my life, scatter by fire, in the name of Jesus.

102. Evil force fighting me with the smoke of disgrace, die by fire, in Jesus' name.

103. Rain of fire, kill every smoke of darkness assigned to frustrate my destiny, in the name of Jesus.

104. Evil price paid to torment my existence, be cancelled by the blood of Jesus, in the name of Jesus.

105. Wicked elders keeping the results of my prayers away from me, release them and die, in the name of Jesus.

106. Powers hiding in the smoke to scatter my joy, be terminated now, in the name of Jesus.

107. Evil smoke distracting me from the way of my blessings, expire by fire, in the name of Jesus.

108. Smoke of darkness blinding my eyes from claiming my blessings, expire, in the name of Jesus.

109. Powers using strange smoke to put my life in bondage, receive the judgement of death, in the name of Jesus.

110. Powers using evil birds to sing songs of curse for me, thunder of God, strike them to death, in the name of Jesus.

111. You my life, carry fire to consume my problems, in the name of Jesus.

112. Battles that have known my name, your time is up, die, in the name of Jesus.

Day 5 (22-09-21) - *The Bible in 70 Days (Day 45- Jeremiah 25:24-43:4)*
Devotional Songs (Pages 4-10)
Praise and Worship
Prayers of Praise and Thanksgiving (Page 13)

113. Smoke of the wicked elders rising at the edge of my miracles, scatter by fire, in the name of Jesus.

114. Powers using animal excreta to pollute my glory, run mad and die, in the name of Jesus.

115. Powers using the excreta of demonic animals to plant hatred into my destiny, run mad and die, in the name of Jesus.

116. Powers pushing me to borrow and not be able to pay back, be disappointed by fire, in the name of Jesus.

117. Powers adding rejection to my name, die, in the name of Jesus.

PRAYER BATTLE (2)

118. Every garment I wore that stopped good things from happening in my life, catch fire, in the name of Jesus.

119. Every problem reducing my life to mockery, die, in the name of Jesus.

120. Misfortune and tragedy sleeping and waking with me, leave my life alone and die, in the name of Jesus.

121. Every battle that is a thorn in my flesh, O God, arise and kill it now, in the name of Jesus.

122. In the house of suffering in which I am, O God, arise and bring me out, in the name of Jesus.

123. Wherever I have been tied down like a cow, angel of the living God, set me free, in the name of Jesus.

124. Powers that say I should use my glory in the grave, be suddenly wasted by fire, in the name of Jesus.

125. What the enemies plan to disgrace me with, O God, arise and use it to promote me, in the name of Jesus.

126. Battles I know nothing about that are attacking me secretly, be disgraced by fire, in the name of Jesus.

127. Silent enemies and silent battles attacking me secretly, be exposed and be disgraced by fire, in the name of Jesus.

128. Inherited battles which are still active in my life, be offloaded by fire, in the name of Jesus.

129. Every evil covenant strengthening battles in my life, be broken by the blood of Jesus, in the name of Jesus.

130. Satanic covenant following me anywhere I go, break, in the name of Jesus.

131. Satanic champion of my father's house, supervising any affliction in my life, fall flat and die, in the name of Jesus.

132. Any problem that has vowed to waste my life, expire by fire, in Jesus' name.

133. Satanic personality that has gone on evil training to waste my destiny, you shall not return, in the name of Jesus.

134. Every license used by the enemies to operate in my life, expire by fire, in the name of Jesus.

135. Strange battles that have vowed to escort me to the grave, be separated from me by fire, in the name of Jesus.

136. Strange shadows in charge of my case, disappear by fire, in Jesus' name.

137. Powers that want me to die by mistake, die in my place, in Jesus' name.

138. Witches and wizards in my family that say that I must not live, die, in the name Jesus.

139. Any evil personality speaking to the sand at night to work against me, die with your sand, in the name of Jesus.

140. My angel of deliverance, appear now and do your work, in the name of Jesus.

Day 6 (23-09-21) - *The Bible in 70 Days (Day 46-Jer 43:5-52:34; Lam 1:1-5:3)*
Devotional Songs (Pages 4-10)
Praise and Worship
Prayers of Praise and Thanksgiving (Page 13)

141. O you grave, vomit my caged blessings , in the name of Jesus.

142. Every satanically empowered thought against me, scatter, in Jesus' name.

143. Long time pains in my life, disappear by fire now, in the name of Jesus.

144. Ancestral evil bird, become deaf and dumb forever concerning my destiny, in the name of Jesus.

145. Evil bird perching on my glory, somersault and die by fire, in Jesus' name.

146. Spiritual evil bird assigned to suck the honey of my life, die, in Jesus' name.

147. Any satanic herbalist preparing charms for my enemies, run mad, in the name of Jesus.

148. The laughter of my enemies over me shall make them run mad, in the name of Jesus.

149. O God, let what gives my enemies peace against me turn to tragedy, in the name of Jesus.

150. Battles making sure that I remain as I am presently, die, in Jesus' name.

151. Destiny killers, destiny swallowers and destiny kidnappers, loose me and let me go , in the name of Jesus.

152. My original glory in the belly of a serpent, angel of the living God, go and bring it out anyhow, in the name of Jesus.

PRAYER BATTLE (2)

153. Powers that hate my existence, die, in the name of Jesus.

154. My hidden enemies, be silenced by the violent angels of God, in Jesus' name.

155. Angels of the living God, go and give my enemies serious plagues that will permanently silence them, in the name of Jesus.

156. Wherever my destiny is hidden, you my angel go now and search it out for me, in the name of Jesus.

157. Any negative condition in my life, mocking my God, die, in Jesus' name.

158. Any affliction hiding in my life, be purged out now by fire, in Jesus' name.

159. Any day in this year marked as my day of death, become the day of celebration, in the name of Jesus.

160. Arrows of death hanging on me, backfire now, in the name of Jesus.

161. Battles that want to swallow my destiny, swallow fire and die, in the name of Jesus.

162. Any agreement between my parents and the devil concerning my life, break by the power in the blood of Jesus, in the name of Jesus.

163. Killers of testimonies, what are you living for? Die by fire, in Jesus' name.

164. Satanic arrows hiding in my body, O mercy of God, bring them out, in the name of Jesus.

165. I command sorrow to visit and live with my stubborn enemies, in the name of Jesus.

166. Powers that say my glory will not manifest while they are alive, die suddenly, in the name of Jesus.

167. Powers cursing me to go from one battle to another battle, O God, silence them with death, in the name of Jesus.

168. Battle against my going out and coming in, scatter by fire, in Jesus' name.

Day 7 (24-09-21) - *The Bible in 70 Days (Day 47 - Lam 5:4 - Ezek 1:1 - 19:8)*
Devotional Songs (Pages 4-10)
Praise and Worship
Prayers of Praise and Thanksgiving (Page 13)

169. Battle of poverty from the highest order, leave my life alone and die, in the name of Jesus.

170. Powers using my life for deadly labour, lose your power over me now, in the name of Jesus.

171. Every periodic problem wasting my life, die, in the name of Jesus.

172. Powers manipulating my head to confuse my helpers, die, in Jesus' name.

173. Strangers hiding to cause havoc in my destiny, leave my life alone and die, in the name of Jesus.

174. Every garment putting me in unwanted situations, catch fire, in Jesus' name.

175. Arrows assigned to make my life the same, without being blessed, scatter by fire, in the name of Jesus.

176. Evil record the enemy kept against my future, catch fire, in Jesus' name.

177. Every satanic follow-up against my life, scatter by fire, in the name of Jesus.

178. Powers joining me to demons by force, lose your power over me, in the name of Jesus.

179. Furnace of darkness disturbing my peace, expire, in the name of Jesus.

180. Powers of demonic furnace assigned to afflict me, backfire, in Jesus' name.

181. Time table of demonic disaster arranged against me, catch fire, in the name of Jesus.

182. Garment of disaster sewn for me, backfire, in the name of Jesus.

183. Thrones of water spirit fashioned against my head, catch fire, in Jesus' name

184. Battles of errors assigned to block me from moving forward, die, in the name of Jesus.

185. Every blocked way to my breakthrough, open by fire, in the name of Jesus.

186. Spirit of disappointment following me in the journey of my life, fire of God, separate us, in the name of Jesus.

187. Spirit of disappointment, leave my life, in the name of Jesus.

188. All the covenants of disappointment over my life, blood of Jesus, destroy them, in the name of Jesus.

189. Every hand of the wicked causing disappointment in my life, wither, in the name of Jesus.

190. Disappointments that manifest at the junction of my success, catch fire, in the name of Jesus.

191. O God, arise and put an end to the battle of disappointment in my life, in the name of Jesus.

192. O God, arise and let my enemies be disappointed over my case, in the name of Jesus.

193. Source of bitterness in my life, dry up, in the name of Jesus.

194. Battle against my joy of great measure, scatter, in the name of Jesus.

195. Cry of agony in my life, stop by fire, in the name of Jesus.

196. Powers helping my enemies to prepare strange arrows against me, use them against yourselves and die, in the name of Jesus.

Day 8 (25-09-21) - *The Bible in 70 Days (Day 48- Ezekiel 19:9 - 34:20)*
Devotional Songs (Pages 4-10)
Praise and Worship
Prayers of Praise and Thanksgiving (Page 13)

197. Strange helpers of my enemies, consume your instruments and die, in the name of Jesus.

198. Powers seeking a stronger power against me, O God, arise and release Your thunder against them, in the name of Jesus.

199. Embargo of demonic cooperation against me, scatter, in the name of Jesus.

200. Witchcraft tailor sewing a garment of tears for me, wear your garment and die, in the name of Jesus.

201. Wicked powers assigned to make my life an example of a bad story, die, in the name of Jesus.

202. Ancient pot of darkness cooking the glory of my life, scatter by fire, in the name of Jesus.

203. Helpers to my enemies, become a trap to them, in the name of Jesus.

204. Angry enemies consuming my virtues, leave my life alone and be wasted, in the name of Jesus.

205. O God, arise and clothe me with the garment that can kill disappointments, in the name of Jesus.

206. Powers using charm to put me into a trap, die, in the name of Jesus.

207. Wicked elders that say I will continue to fight without solution, O God, judge them quickly, in the name of Jesus.

208. Every strange goat of my father's house, appearing in my dream, catch fire, in the name of Jesus.

209. I attack and render useless the eyes of every witchcraft animal on a mission to plant evil against me, in the name of Jesus.

210. O God, deliver my soul from the spirit of animals, in the name of Jesus.

211. Any power that is using a bird to drag my destiny to the ground, fall down and die, in the name of Jesus.

212. Household animals troubling my life, go back to your sender, in Jesus' name.

213. Witchdoctor animals assigned against my destiny, catch fire, in Jesus' name.

214. Every satanic instruction given to any animal to eliminate me, backfire, in the name of Jesus.

215. My glory shall not be given to animals to feed on, in the name of Jesus.

216. Satanic lion's den prepared for me and my family, swallow your owners, in the name of Jesus.

217. Warrior angels of God, arise in the war front of the wicked elders against me and destroy them, in the name of Jesus.

218. O God, arise and keep my enemies busy with what will destroy them, in the name of Jesus.

219. Every consuming weapon of the enemy against me, backfire, in Jesus' name.

220. Every evil hand dropping problems into my life, wither by fire, in the name of Jesus.

221. Powers stepping on my pictures to curse me, receive the arrow of death, in the name of Jesus.

222. Whoever is close to me and is holding my peace, lose your power over me, in the name of Jesus.

223. Any dangerous sacrifice made on my behalf, catch fire, in the name of Jesus.

224. Visitation of darkness into my life, backfire, in the name of Jesus.

Day 9 (26-09-21) - *The Bible in 70 Days (Day 49 - Eze 34:21 - Dan 1:1 -2:19)*

Devotional Songs (Pages 4-10)

Praise and Worship

Prayers of Praise and Thanksgiving (Page 13)

225. Every property of the enemy in my life, catch fire, in the name of Jesus.

226. Visitors of the night assigned to disgrace me, die, in the name of Jesus.

227. Terror by night threatening my life locate your senders, in the name of Jesus.
228. Arrows that flieth by day, locate your senders, in the name of Jesus.
229. Pestilence that walketh in darkness, locate you senders, in Jesus' name.
230. Every bird of witchcraft assigned to trouble my progress, you are a liar, die, in the name of Jesus.
231. Stones of witchcraft fired into my life, locate the head of your senders, in the name of Jesus.
232. Every curse of 'this is how far you can go', issued against my life, break, in the name of Jesus.
233. Every secret of my life in wrong hands, be wiped off by the blood of Jesus, in the name of Jesus.
234. Foundational battles fought by my parents, that are repeating themselves in my life, die, in the name of Jesus.
235. Thou power of God, disgrace the laughter of my enemies, in Jesus' name.
236. Powers that have vowed to tear my destiny to pieces, Lion of the tribe of Judah, tear them to pieces, in the name of Jesus.
237. Enemies of my progress, wherever you are, receive the beating of God, in the name of Jesus.
238. Powers destroying my joy every month, O God, waste them, in Jesus' name.
239. Ancestral powers that want me to die in battle, O God, arise and kill them, in the name of Jesus.
240. Satanic bullets lodging in my body, what are you waiting for? Backfire, in the name of Jesus.
241. All evil kings and queens, cursing my life and destiny from my root, die without remedy, in the name of Jesus.
242. Witchcraft war from the wicked elders against me, scatter by fire, in the name of Jesus.
243. Any strong curse following my life around to make my life miserable, blood of Jesus, break it now, in the name of Jesus.
244. O God, arise and disgrace my blackmailers, in the name of Jesus.
245. Unsettled spirits troubling my destiny, die, in the name of Jesus.
246. Killers inside my destiny, die, in the name of Jesus.
247. Fire of God, fight every stranger in my destiny, in the name of Jesus.

248.   Evil altar controlling my destiny, catch fire, in the name of Jesus.

249.   Every gift that has killed my virtues, mercy of God help me to recover it, in the name of Jesus.

250.   Anyone in my family, secretly working against me, be disappointed, in the name of Jesus.

251.   Any spirit feeding my problems against me, thunder of God, send it away from me, in the name of Jesus.

252.   You battle on a death assignment against me, die, in the name of Jesus.

Day 10 (27-09-21) - *The Bible in 70 Days (Day 50 - Dan 2:20 - Hos 1:1-9:13)*

Devotional Songs (Pages 4-10)

Praise and Worship

Prayers of Praise and Thanksgiving (Page 13)

253.   Whosoever is using the wind to attack me, die, in the name of Jesus.

254.   Whosoever has sent a message to herbalist to fight me, receive the anger of God, in the name of Jesus.

255.   Whosoever is using the ground to fight me, O God, arise and fight against him, in the name of Jesus.

256.   Powers making me to struggle for what belongs to me, die, in Jesus' name.

257.   Fire of God, swallow those that hate me, in the name of Jesus.

258.   Whoever buried my garment to kill me, die, in the name of Jesus.

259.   O God, let the charms that my enemies depend on kill them, in Jesus' name.

260.   My enemies shall be afraid to call my name, in the name of Jesus.

261.   Every curse that has closed my destiny, die, in the name of Jesus.

262.   O God, arise and let my enemies disappoint their pillars, in Jesus' name.

263.   The arrow that the enemy wants to send against me, let him send it to his herbalists, in the name of Jesus.

264.   Battles crying against my destiny, I silence you by fire, in the name of Jesus.

265.   Strange pot in a strange tree, fighting me, catch fire, in the name of Jesus.

266.   Evil stones of the enemies thrown against me, backfire, in the name of Jesus.

267.   Pit of the enemies, kill the enemies, in the name of Jesus.

268.   The arrows that will create problem in the camp of my enemies, O God, send

them to my enemies, in the name of Jesus.

269. O God, arise and destroy the confidence of my enemies against me, in the name of Jesus.

270. Power eyeing my seat of glory for evil, go blind, in the name of Jesus.

271. Powers conniving with diabolical powers to bring me down, die, in the name of Jesus.

272. Powers ganging up wickedly to disgrace me, scatter, in the name of Jesus.

273. Hands joining hands to waste me, destroy yourselves, in the name of Jesus.

274. Powers that want to kill me by accident, receive the arrow of death, in the name of Jesus.

275. Powers assigned to use my destiny to test their charms, be wasted, in the name of Jesus.

276. In my glory, dancing and singing shall not die, in the name of Jesus.

277. Powers assigned to force me to sit down in shame, receive the arrow of disappointment, in the name of Jesus.

278. Brass in my heaven, melt away by fire, in the name of Jesus.

279. Wherever my enemies are hiding, O God, arise and bring them down, in the name of Jesus.

280. Any garment of darkness releasing sickness into my life, be consumed by fire, in the name of Jesus.

SECTION CONFESSIONS

In the name of Jesus Christ, I hand over all my battles to the Lord Jesus Christ. The Lord fights for me and I hold my peace. I am an overcomer through the name of Jesus Christ. I am victorious in all circumstances and situations that are against me, in Jesus' name. Jesus Christ has defeated all my enemies, and they are brought down and fallen under my feet, in the name of Jesus. I crush them all to the ground and I command them to begin to lick up the dust of the earth under my feet; for, at the name of Jesus, every knee must bow, in the name of Jesus. When I call upon the name of the Lord, He shall stretch forth His mighty hand and lift me above all my enemies and deliver me from all of them, in the name of Jesus.

PRAYER BATTLE (2)

In the name of Jesus, I am inscribed in the palm of God's mighty hand. I am neatly tucked away and hidden from all the evils and troubles of this present world, in the name of Jesus. Henceforth, I refuse to live in fear. Rather, my fear and dread shall be upon all my enemies. As soon as they hear of me, they shall submit themselves to me, in Jesus' name. God wishes above all things that I prosper, in Jesus' name. I receive prosperity, in Jesus' name. God has not given me the spirit of bondage, to fear. The word of God is quick and powerful in my mouth. God has put the power of His word in my mouth, in the name of Jesus. I am not a failure; I shall operate at the head only and not beneath, in the name of Jesus.

SECTION VIGIL

(To be done at night between the hours of 12 midnight and 2 am)

HYMN FOR THE VIGIL (Pages 10-11)

1. Whatever form of satanic diversion that has been planned for me and my family, backfire, in the name of Jesus.

2. I come against any kind of sudden disaster hiding in the dark against me, in the name of Jesus.

3. Powers giving me strange battles to waste my life, run mad and die, in the name of Jesus.

4. Powers of the wicked elders, assigned to make me find myself in troubles instead of celebration, O God, arise and judge them quickly, in Jesus' name.

5. Every demonic apprentice, using my destiny as a tool for attacks, die suddenly, in the name of Jesus.

6. Powers sending problems to me whenever I want to move forward, die with your load, in the name of Jesus.

7. Any sickness programmed into my body to stop my progress, die, in the name of Jesus.

8. Any power that has locked me up, release me by thunder, in Jesus' name.

9. Any power struggling to close the door of my goodness, be disgraced, in the name of Jesus.

10. Every mark of 'you shall not experience success', placed upon my destiny,

blood of Jesus, wash them away, in the name of Jesus.

11. Powers terminating good things that have been convenient for me, be wasted, in the name of Jesus.

12. Any power preventing people from blessing me, be paralysed, in Jesus' name.

13. Any battle assigned to close the door of my joy, die, in the name of Jesus.

14. Every mouth spoiling my testimony, catch fire, in the name of Jesus.

15. Any mouth chanting against my testimony, be silenced by fire, in Jesus' name.

16. Lion of the tribe of Judah, arise, destroy my testimony killers now, in the name of Jesus.

17. Testimony killers, hear the word of the Lord, I sentence you to compulsory madness, in the name of Jesus.

18. O God of vengeance, arise, visit the enemies of my testimonies with Your anger, in the name of Jesus.

19. Every enemy of my multiple testimonies, receive divine bullet, in Jesus' name.

20. O God, arise and let my testimony shock my friends and surprise my enemies, in the name of Jesus.

21. Any power going to any length to use magic and charms against me, run mad and die, in the name of Jesus.

SECTION 6 - SCATTER THE SCATTERERS

Scripture Reading: Psalms 35

Confession: Isaiah 8:9-10: Associate yourselves, O ye people, and ye shall be broken in pieces; and give ear, all ye of far countries: gird yourselves, and ye shall be broken in pieces; gird yourselves, and ye shall be broken in pieces. Take counsel together, and it shall come to nought; speak the word, and it shall not stand: for God is with us.

Day 1(28-09-21) - *The Bible in 70 Days (Day 51 - Hos 9:14 - Mic 1:1-7:1)*

Devotional Songs (Pages 4-10)

Praise and Worship

Prayers of Praise and Thanksgiving (Page 13)

1. O God, arise and let the pride of my enemies put them to shame, in the name of Jesus.

2. Powers pushing me away from my divine helpers, die, in the name of Jesus.

3. My head, refuse to cooperate with the enemy of my destiny, in Jesus' name.

4. Powers that have vowed that I will waste my time praying, die, in Jesus' name.

5. Power saying I will waste the time of my life in battle, O God, arise and judge them quickly, in the name of Jesus.

6. Powers assigned to put my way forward in darkness, you are failures, die, in the name of Jesus.

7. O God, make my name poisonous in the mouth of my enemies, in Jesus' name.

8. O God, arise and break the confidence of the wicked elders against me, in the name of Jesus.

9. Every material of disgrace in my destiny, catch fire, in the name of Jesus.

10. Mercy of God, cover my mistakes, in the name of Jesus.

11. Powers using my testimony against me, die, in the name of Jesus.

12. Powers assigned to close my mouth so as to close my destiny, die, in the name of Jesus.

13. Powers making things difficult for my helpers, die, in the name of Jesus.

14. Every wicked prophet mandated to trouble me, die, in the name of Jesus.

15. Powers invoking the dead to pursue me, thunder of God, strike them to death, in the name of Jesus.

16. Powers burying my name with the dead, die a shameful death, in Jesus' name.

17. The enemy of change to my unpleasant condition will not kill me, by the power in the blood of Jesus, in the name of Jesus.

18. Every bad song from the womb that is affecting my life, catch fire, in the name of Jesus.

19. Curses holding me where I don't belong, break and let me go, in Jesus' name.

20. Powers saying 'no' to the 'yes' of God in my life, die, in the name of Jesus.

21. I shall not die in my problem, in the name of Jesus.

22. O God, arise and turn the celebration of darkness for my sake to mourning, in the name of Jesus.

23. Strange name given to me from the kingdom of darkness, I reject you, in the name of Jesus.

24. Terrible mat of darkness wrapping my virtues, release it and catch fire, in the name of Jesus.

25. Strange call of darkness assigned to trap me, expire by fire, in Jesus' name

26. Powers assigned to kill me through strange call, die, in the name of Jesus.

27. Strange call on assignment to steal my joy, I silence you, in the name of Jesus.

28. Evil call assigned to unclothe me, be silenced by fire, in the name of Jesus.

Day 2 (29-09-21) - *The Bible in 70 Days (Day 52-Micah 7:2 - Malachi 1:1-2:6)*
Devotional Songs (Pages 4-10)
Praise and Worship
Prayers of Praise and Thanksgiving (Page 13)

29. Evil call assigned to make me run mad, die, in the name of Jesus.

30. Evil call assigned to force me to make mistakes that will put me in trouble, clear away by fire, in the name of Jesus.

31. Evil call assigned to place evil crown on my head, become dumb, in the name of Jesus.

32. Evil call assigned to make me run away from my helpers, I silence you, in the name of Jesus.

PRAYER BATTLE (2)

33. Evil call assigned to sacrifice my destiny, scatter, in the name of Jesus.

34. Evil call assigned to separate me from God, become permanently silenced, in the name of Jesus.

35. Evil call assigned to send arrow into my life, die, in the name of Jesus.

36. Family demon frustrating my destiny, depart from me, in the name of Jesus.

37. O God, arise and disgrace every trap of poverty in my life, in the name of Jesus.

38. Battles against every work that I do, die, in the name of Jesus.

39. I recover my joy from the cage of wicked people, in the name of Jesus.

40. Spirit behind my family battle, die, in the name of Jesus.

41. You, work of my hands, reject the mark of poverty, in the name of Jesus.

42. Battles arranged to hold me down, scatter by fire, in the name of Jesus.

43. Evil blood bank requesting for my blood, catch fire, in the name of Jesus.

44. Every problem that will make me to beg from those I should bless, I reject you by fire, in the name of Jesus.

45. My life shall not attract and befriend battles, in the name of Jesus.

46. Poison of darkness assigned to kill my joy, be terminated by the blood of Jesus, in the name of Jesus.

47. Property of darkness in my destiny, catch fire, in the name of Jesus.

48. I crush the heads of the wicked elders fighting against me, in Jesus' name.

49. O God, create a wall of fire between me and any evil, in the name of Jesus.

50. Evil call putting me in a strange situation, scatter by fire, in the name of Jesus.

51. Powers sustaining their evil purpose against me, swallow your evil purpose and die, in the name of Jesus.

52. O God, scatter the tongue of the wicked against me, in the name of Jesus.

53. O Lord, deliver me from the gathering of evil broadcasters, in Jesus' name.

54. Demonic prophecy coming to pass in my life, I stop you by fire, in Jesus' name.

55. Evil progress of the enemies in my life, I stop you by fire, in the name of Jesus.

56. Lord, deliver my tongue from becoming a cemetery of evil, in Jesus' name.

PRAYER BATTLE (2)

Day 3 (30-09-21) - *The Bible in 70 Days (Day 53 - Mal 2:7 - Matt 1:1-13:13)*

Devotional Songs (Pages 4-10)

Praise and Worship

Prayers of Praise and Thanksgiving (Page 13)

57. Every acidic arrow fired into my life, backfire, in the name of Jesus.
58. O Lord, paralyse and nullify the activities of jungle and vagabond spirits in my life, in the name of Jesus.
59. Lord, let there be a civil war in the kingdom of darkness working against my rising and shining, in the name of Jesus.
60. Every demonic doorkeeper locking out good things from me, be paralysed by fire, in the name of Jesus.
61. I disobey satanic order against my joy, in the name of Jesus.
62. Lord, let the finger, vengeance, terror, anger, fear, wrath, hatred and burning judgement of God be released against my full time enemies, in Jesus' name.
63. Every stronghold of darkness caging my destiny receive acidic confusion, in the name of Jesus.
64. O God, arise and put the mouth of my enemies to the dust, in Jesus' name.
65. Every demonic claim of the earth over my life, be dismantled, in Jesus' name.
66. O Lord, when my enemies cry to You, shut out their cries, in the name of Jesus.
67. Glory of serpentine enemies reigning over my destiny, be terminated, in the name of Jesus.
68. Anyone going to the shrine to send me the gift of disgrace, carry your gift and die, in the name of Jesus.
69. Evil arrows that fly everywhere will not locate me and my family, in the name of Jesus.
70. Every call of shame in my life, die, in the name of Jesus.
71. The powers of the strong man will not grip my destiny unawares, in the name of Jesus.
72. Anywhere my name is being mentioned for evil, fire of God, fight for me, in the name of Jesus.
73. Every satanic voice limiting the scope of my destiny, shut up and be silenced forever, in the name of Jesus.
74. My spirit man, jump out of the meeting point of my enemies, in Jesus' name.

75. Every idolatrous voice speaking against my moving forward, shut up and die, in the name of Jesus.

76. Every chapter of battle in my life, catch fire, in the name of Jesus.

77. O God, use me to bring solution to the problem in my family and announce my destiny, in the name of Jesus.

78. Evil midnight calabash placed in any crossroad against my life, catch fire, in the name of Jesus.

79. I destroy by fire, every boundary the enemy has marked down for me, in the name of Jesus.

80. Anyone who has paid money to an evil shrine to destroy my life, run mad and die, in the name of Jesus.

81. O Lord, fix what You have originally purposed for my life, for my situation to be fixed, in the name of Jesus.

82. Any hand behind my affliction, break to pieces, in the name of Jesus.

83. O God, arise and release Your judgement on all the enemies of my life, in the name of Jesus.

84. Every pot of darkness placed upon my destiny, break by fire, in Jesus' name.

Day 4 (01-10-21) - *The Bible in 70 Days (Day 54-Matthew 13:14 - 24:39)*

Devotional Songs (Pages 4-10)

Praise and Worship

Prayers of Praise and Thanksgiving (Page 13)

85. O God, arise and destroy every hindrance in my life, in the name of Jesus.

86. Dark powers seeking my shame, die in shame for my sake, in Jesus' name.

87. In the name of Jesus, I shall not eat the bread of sorrow; I shall not eat the bread of shame; I shall not eat the bread of defeat.

88. Rivers of darkness spreading problems into my life, dry up and die, in the name of Jesus.

89. Any garment of darkness releasing sickness into my life, be consumed by fire, in the name of Jesus.

90. Every satanic joy over any problem that I have, turn to mourning, in the name of Jesus.

91. Every evil arrow fired into my destiny, fire of God, burn it to ashes, in the name

of Jesus.

92. Lord, let the sun of destruction consume all my tormentors, in Jesus' name.

93. Any information about me that the enemy is using to afflict me, thunder of God, destroy it, in the name of Jesus.

94. Anyone visiting the crossroad to curse me, run mad and die, in Jesus' name.

95. Powers replacing my garment of glory with the garment of shame, return my garment of glory to me and die, in the name of Jesus.

96. Powers that have vowed to make frustration my food, O God, arise and beat them to death, in the name of Jesus.

97. Powers that are boasting that they would see how God will save me, O God, arise and bury them, in the name of Jesus.

98. Any power assigned to marry me to a strange captivity, die, in Jesus' name.

99. Every problem from the realm of darkness, making me to walk into cobwebs, be destroyed by fire, in the name of Jesus.

100. O my Rock and my Strong Tower, shelter me from the stormy blast of the enemies, in the name of Jesus.

101. O heavens, hear the voice of the Lord, gather yourselves together and promote me, in the name of Jesus.

102. Every gap between my minimum breakthrough and my potential maximum breakthrough, close, in the name of Jesus.

103. Father, turn me into a ball of the Holy Ghost fire which cannot be tormented, in the name of Jesus.

104. Bullets of darkness assigned to turn me to a slave, go back to your senders, in the name of Jesus.

105. Every satanic power using evil night to strangulate my destiny, catch fire, in the name of Jesus.

106. Anyone carrying sacrifices to waste my life, be wasted, in the name of Jesus.

107. Blood of Jesus, hide me from secret enemies, today and forever, in the name of Jesus.

108. Powers sending problems to me whenever I want to move forward, die with your load, in the name of Jesus.

109. Any sickness programmed into my body to stop my progress, die, in the name of Jesus.

110. Any power that has locked me up, release me by thunder, in Jesus' name.

111. Any power struggling to close the door of my goodness, be disgraced, in the name of Jesus.

112. Any power preventing people from blessing me, be paralysed, in the name of Jesus.

Day 5 (02-10-21) - *The Bible in 70 Days (Day 55-Matt 24:40 - Mark 1:1 - 6:33)*

Devotional Songs (Pages 4-10)

Praise and Worship

Prayers of Praise and Thanksgiving (Page 13)

113. Any battle assigned to close the door of my joy, die, in the name of Jesus.

114. Every mouth spoiling my testimony, catch fire, in the name of Jesus.

115. Any mouth chanting against my testimony, be silenced by fire, in the name of Jesus.

116. Lion of the tribe of Judah, arise, destroy my testimony killers now, in the name of Jesus.

117. Testimony killers, hear the word of the Lord, I sentence you to compulsory madness, in the name of Jesus.

118. O God of vengeance, arise, visit the enemies of my testimonies with Your anger, in the name of Jesus.

119. O God, arise and let my testimony shock my friends and surprise my enemies, in the name of Jesus.

120. Every wall of darkness around me, angel of God, break it, in Jesus' name.

121. Kingdom of darkness resurrecting dead battles in my life, thunder of God scatter it, in the name of Jesus.

122. Wicked powers assigned to waste my life in battle, die, in the name of Jesus.

123. Powers placing battles in my hand, carry your load and die, in Jesus' name.

124. O God, arise and disappoint any man working with satan to destroy my life, in the name of Jesus.

125. Any strange mark polluting my destiny, return to your sender with his evil

PRAYER BATTLE (2)

intentions, in the name of Jesus.

126. Destruction, fall upon all powers giving me bad dreams, in the name of Jesus.

127. Every power raging to make me poor, die by fire, in the name of Jesus.

128. Powers drawing strength from the sun and the moon against me, O Lord, disgrace them, in the name of Jesus.

129. O God, arise and withdraw the weapons of my enemies, in Jesus' name.

130. Arrows that will make people shake their heads in pity for me, go back to your senders, in the name of Jesus.

131. Wicked powers pouring my blessings away like water, be wasted, in the name of Jesus.

132. O God, draw out Your sword against evil powers preparing me for reproach, in the name of Jesus.

133. Weeping shall not replace laughter in my life, in the name of Jesus.

134. Battles that have vowed to kill me at the end, die, in the name of Jesus.

135. Family battles assigned to bury my head, release my head and die, in the name of Jesus.

136. Any dangerous power from my foundation, holding the keys of my destiny, release them and die, in the name of Jesus.

137. My glory and the lifter of my head, arise and lift me up, in the name of Jesus.

138. Any blood covenant assigned against me, break, in the name of Jesus.

139. Powers increasing my troubles, die, in the name of Jesus.

140. O Lord, let Your voice shake the enemy out of my destiny, in Jesus' name.

Day 6 (03-10-21) - *The Bible in 70 Days (Day 56-Mark 6:34 - 16:11)*
Devotional Songs (Pages 4-10)
Praise and Worship
Prayers of Praise and Thanksgiving (Page 13)

141. O Lord, deliver my finances from the control of darkness, in Jesus' name.

142. All the traps that the enemies set to rob me, scatter, in the name of Jesus.

143. Powers feeding me with the food of battles, eat your food and die, in the name of Jesus.

144. Every false witness rising to increase my battle, die, in the name of Jesus.

145. Doors of poverty sent to surround my life, backfire, in the name of Jesus.

146. Any power that hates my celebration, O God, arise and disgrace it, in the name of Jesus.

147. I shall sing the song my enemy does not want me to sing, in Jesus' name.

148. I shall dance the dance my enemy does not want me to dance, in the name of Jesus.

149. Any power that has turned itself to a terror in my life, scatter, in Jesus' name.

150. Powers that used fear to stop my parents and are now pursuing me, die, in the name of Jesus.

151. Any covenant of death threatening my existence, scatter, in Jesus' name.

152. Battles sitting upon my destiny, saying 'you can never go', sword of God, scatter them, in the name of Jesus.

153. Any evil presence locating me every night when I sleep, disappear by fire, in the name of Jesus.

154. Powers assigned to make me to always walk into trouble, die, in the name of Jesus.

155. Any personality hiding in my feet to direct me to the wrong persons, die, in the name of Jesus.

156. Every object buried against my destiny, be uprooted and scatter by fire, in the name of Jesus.

157. Any bitter tree in my life, wither by fire, in the name of Jesus.

158. Every power using altars to war against me, die by fire, in the name of Jesus.

159. Witchcraft powers seeking my death to possess more deadly powers, die suddenly, in the name of Jesus.

160. Occult powers seeking my glory to feed on, run mad and die, in Jesus' name.

161. Anyone that has worn the garment of evil against me, die with your garment, in the name of Jesus.

162. Lord, let Your mercy withdraw me from stubborn wickedness, in the name of Jesus.

163. The garments my enemies are using to cover their shame, catch fire, in the

name of Jesus.

164. O God, arise and let me not fall before my enemies, in the name of Jesus.

165. Powers rejoicing at my tears, die, in the name of Jesus.

166. Dark powers that have vowed to disturb my life, be scattered, in the name of Jesus.

167. Every growing problem in my life, die, in the name of Jesus.

168. Arrows of darkness making my problems to become serious problems, scatter by fire, in the name of Jesus.

Day 7 (04-09-21) - *The Bible in 70 Days (Day 57 - Mak 16:12 - Luk 1:1 - 9:27)*
Devotional Songs (Pages 4-10)
Praise and Worship
Prayers of Praise and Thanksgiving (Page 13)

169. Powers preparing to start my battles all over again, you shall not survive, die suddenly, in the name of Jesus.

170. Powers that want to help my enemies to destroy me, stones of God, kill them, in the name of Jesus.

171. Powers that want me to help my enemies to destroy me, scatter, in the name of Jesus.

172. Powers that want my potential to die with me, be wasted, in Jesus' name.

173. Blood-thirsty demons assigned to eat my flesh and drink my blood, die, in the name of Jesus.

174. Every instrument of darkness used to put me in the den of stagnancy, catch fire, in the name of Jesus.

175. I break every demonic crown upon my head, in the name of Jesus.

176. Every problem that came into my life through the blood of my parents, die, in the name of Jesus.

177. Powers struggling to swallow me, O earth, swallow them, in Jesus' name.

178. The reproach of darkness assigned against me shall not prosper. It shall backfire, in the name of Jesus.

179. Garment of darkness manipulating my destiny, I tear you to pieces, in the name of Jesus.

PRAYER BATTLE (2)

180. You, ancestral strong man standing between me and my destiny, fall down and die, in the name of Jesus.

181. Every soul-tie connecting me to dead people, break by the blood of Jesus, in the name of Jesus.

182. Destiny delay in my life caused by evil dreams, die, in the name of Jesus.

183. Perverted destiny, disappear from my life, in the name of Jesus.

184. Warrior angels of the living God, contend with all the evil angels contending with my life, in the name of Jesus.

185. O stars from heaven, arise and fight my battles from heaven, in Jesus' name.

186. Strong men surrounding me, attack and destroy yourselves, in Jesus' name.

187. Raging and fiery furnace of affliction prepared for me, consume your owners, in the name of Jesus.

188. Sword of envy assigned against me, devour your owner, in Jesus' name.

189. Sword of sorrow, tears and blood assigned against me, be broken to pieces, in the name of Jesus.

190. Sword of poverty and disease assigned against me, I rebuke you by the blood of Jesus, catch fire, in the name of Jesus.

191. O God, arise and sweep away every power fighting my glory, in Jesus' name.

192. Every storm prepared against the ship of my destiny, be silenced, in the name of Jesus.

193. I command angelic slap on every power pulling down my plans and wearing out my prayer knees, in the name of Jesus.

194. Arrows of weak hands, I am not your candidate, backfire, in Jesus' name.

195. O God, arise and deliver the strong city of my destiny into my hands, in the name of Jesus.

196. My legs, hear the word of the Lord, possess your holy mountains by fire, in the name of Jesus.

Day 8 (05-10-21) - *The Bible in 70 Days (Day 58-Luke 9:28 - 19:41)*

Devotional Songs (Pages 4-10)

Praise and Worship

Prayers of Praise and Thanksgiving (Page 13)

197. You treasures of darkness and hidden riches of fortified city, arise by fire, locate me and become mine, in the name of Jesus.

198. Every fortified city harbouring my breakthroughs, let your wall crumble by fire, in the name of Jesus.

199. Power of the Most High, catapult me by fire, in the name of Jesus.

200. Rain of glory, fall upon my life and wash away my shame, in Jesus' name.

201. Rain of breakthroughs, fall upon me and silence my mockers, in Jesus' name.

202. O God, arise and let Your prosperous hand carry me to my throne, in the name of Jesus.

203. Every power occupying my throne of destiny, tremble and vacate my throne, in the name of Jesus.

204. Every face of mockery smiling and laughing at me, receive the stones of fire, in the name of Jesus.

205. Power of sorrow and regret playing games with my life, die, in Jesus' name.

206. Every weapon fashioned to waste my virtues, perish, in the name of Jesus.

207. I trample to death every failure thrown at me by strangers, in Jesus' name.

208. Every stubborn affliction assigned to bury me, die, in the name of Jesus.

209. Every power using the secret of midnight to attack me, sleep and never wake up, in the name of Jesus.

210. Every power multiplying troubles for my life, be consumed by fire, in the name of Jesus.

211. Power of unstoppable testimonies, fall upon my life now, in Jesus' name.

212. My Father, let Your grace terminate my disgrace, in the name of Jesus.

213. Anything in my life feeding my problems, die, in the name of Jesus.

214. Powers using dark prayers to disturb my progress, die, in the name of Jesus.

215. Anyone that wants to quench the fire of my destiny, be terminated, in the

name of Jesus.

216. Tree of darkness holding ancestral records against me, catch fire, in the name of Jesus.

217. Every wicked command from wicked mouth against me, expire, in the name of Jesus.

218. Sacrifices offered to make me lose my destiny, lose your power over me, in the name of Jesus.

219. Powers planting themselves into my life to cause uncommon death, clear out, in the name of Jesus.

220. O God, release Your thunder against any shrine where the glory of my father's house has been sacrificed, in the name of Jesus.

221. Witchcraft powers using cobwebs to sow garments for me, run mad and die, in the name of Jesus.

222. The battles that swallowed my father, you will not shake me, in Jesus' name.

223. Any ancestral mark in my body, attracting demonic birds into my house, expire, in the name of Jesus.

224. Battles fighting against my favour and health, die, in the name of Jesus.

Day 9(06-10-21) - *The Bible in 70 Days (Day 59 - Luk 19:42 - John 1:1 - 5:6)*

Devotional Songs (Pages 4-10)

Praise and Worship

Prayers of Praise and Thanksgiving (Page 13)

225. Every dog of Goliath barking against me, receive the wrath of the living God, in the name of Jesus.

226. Holy Ghost, empower my prayer life, in the name of Jesus.

227. Every known and unknown troubler of my Israel, forcing themselves on me, fight yourselves to death, in the name of Jesus.

228. Every agenda of the wicked elders assigned to make me sick, scatter by fire, in the name of Jesus.

229. O Lord, locate the power house of my problems and set it on fire, in the name of Jesus.

230. Powers sitting on the throne of my testimonies, be choked and die, in the

name of Jesus.

231. Battle extenders, success robbers, depart from my life by fire, in the name of Jesus.

232. Powers assigned to punish my source of income, receive the judgement of God and die, in the name of Jesus.

233. Arrows making me to see troubles and battles on every side, go back to your senders, in the name of Jesus.

234. Powers tying me down to any situation that does not glorify God, leave my life alone, in the name of Jesus.

235. Every dog of darkness fighting for my glory, die, in the name of Jesus.

236. I will not kiss Delilah; I will not wash the feet of Jezebel; I will not hug Judas; I will not honour Gehazi, in the name of Jesus.

237. Brothers of Joseph in my father's house, scatter by fire, in the name of Jesus.

238. Powers weakening my helpers, die, in the name of Jesus.

239. Witchcraft hands placed over my eyes, wither by fire, in the name of Jesus.

240. Evil chains around my blessings, break by fire, in the name of Jesus.

241. Powers of Herod working against my breakthroughs, die, in Jesus' name.

242. Battles celebrating every birthday with me, be terminated, in Jesus' name.

243. Father, clear away every traffic of frustration delaying my celebration, in the name of Jesus.

244. Wicked elders using the dust to waste my joy and blessings, O Lord, waste them, in the name of Jesus.

245. Battles assigned to dry up my oil of favour, scatter by fire, in Jesus' name.

246. I shall not wander away from my wonders, in the name of Jesus.

247. Father, make my voice a rod to divide the Red Sea ahead of me, in the name of Jesus.

248. O God, arise and command the proud waters that surround my life to dry up, in the name of Jesus.

249. Blood of Jesus, cover me as a garment, soak me as a flood, surround me as wall against my enemies, in the name of Jesus.

250. My feet, my feet, my feet, hear the word of the Lord, refuse to run errands

of losses and crises, in the name of Jesus.

251. Powers preparing rooms for me in prisons, enter your rooms and die there, in the name of Jesus.

252. I shall not beg my enemies; I shall not run errand for darkness, in the name of Jesus.

Day 10 (07-10-21) - *The Bible in 70 Days (Day 60-John 5:7 - 13:30)*
Devotional Songs (Pages 4-10)
Praise and Worship
Prayers of Praise and Thanksgiving (Page 13)

253. I raise an altar of daily trouble against robbers around my destiny, in the name of Jesus.

254. Lord, destroy every investment of the enemy in every area of my life, in the name of Jesus.

255. Lord, build Your tower of power around my glory, in the name of Jesus.

256. Powers threatening me that celebration can never be my portion, receive angelic slap, in the name of Jesus.

257. Every power assigned to backstab me, stab yourself to death, in the name of Jesus.

258. Strange battles assigned to bring me back into bondage, die, in Jesus' name.

259. Powers creating problems and strange situations for me, Rock of Ages, grind them to powder, in the name of Jesus.

260. Every destiny and glory robber riding on the horse of my destiny, somersault and die, in the name of Jesus.

261. Judges of darkness seeking for my death, run mad and die, in Jesus' name.

262. Dark powers assigned to make me a bad story when I am still alive, O God, arise and judge them quickly, in the name of Jesus.

263. Sudden problems, unexpected problems assigned to mock me, scatter by fire, in the name of Jesus.

264. Strange battles assigned to mess me up, mock my destiny and frustrate my efforts, scatter, in the name of Jesus.

265. Strange battles assigned to mess up my talents, mock my destiny and

frustrate my efforts, scatter by fire, in the name of Jesus.

266. Battle of strange tongues raging against my lifting and success, catch fire, in the name of Jesus.

267. Any battle in my life asking for my God, bow to the name of Jesus, in the name of Jesus.

268. Destiny-crippling battles, leave my life alone and die, in the name of Jesus.

269. The secret behind the battles that are against my life, O God, arise, expose them and destroy them, in the name of Jesus.

270. Every power that does not want to see me around, your time is up, fall down and die, in the name of Jesus.

271. Any satanic bird crying to kill me, receive the arrow of death, in Jesus' name.

272. Battles assigned to grow up with me, die by fire, in the name of Jesus.

273. Battles blocking my prayers, scatter and die, in the name of Jesus.

274. Powers using strange power to harass me constantly, run mad and die, in the name of Jesus.

275. Every demon transferred from my parents to frustrate me, be consumed by fire, in the name of Jesus.

276. Terrible captivity of my father's house, assigned to make my glory a history while I am still living, thunder of God, scatter it, in the name of Jesus.

277. Power attacking and insulting me, thunder of God, beat it to death, in the name of Jesus.

278. O God, arise and curse all my secret troubles to die, in the name of Jesus.

279. Battle of irregular favour satanically assigned against me, die, in the name of Jesus.

280. Battles assigned to expose me to shame before I can get a little favour, die, in the name of Jesus.

SECTION CONFESSIONS

I trust in the word of God. The word stands sure when I speak it; it will accomplish the purpose for which I have spoken it, in Jesus' name. I am the manifestation, the product and the result of God's word. God has spoken into my life and I have become the manifested presence of Jehovah God on earth. I expressly manifest everything the word of God says I am. I am filled with the word of life. Because the Lord disappointeth the devices of the crafty so that their hands cannot perform their enterprise, every work of the strong, the wicked, the evil and the enemy against my life shall not prosper, in the name of Jesus. In the name of Jesus, I claim the power in the name of the Lord to overcome all the troops of the enemy. In the name of Jesus Christ, by the presence of God in my life, I command the wicked to perish before me; and melt away like wax in the fire. I am a child of God, I am dwelling in the secret place of the Most High God; I am protected and covered under the shadow of the wings of Jehovah, in the name of Jesus.

The word of God is the power of God, and the entrance of the word of God into my life has brought the light of God into my life and darkness cannot comprehend it, in the name of Jesus. I send forth this light that is in me as a two-edged sword to destroy all the kingdoms of darkness, in the name of Jesus. The word of God is quick and powerful in my mouth. God has put the power of His word in my mouth, in the name of Jesus.

SECTION VIGIL

(To be done at night between the hours of 12 midnight and 2 am)

HYMN FOR THE VIGIL (Pages 10-11)

1. Any power using any evil means to steal from me, be destroyed by fire, in the name of Jesus.

2. Every wall of darkness around me, angel of God, break it, in the name of Jesus.

3. Kingdom of darkness arising dead battles in my life, thunder of God scatter them, in the name of Jesus.

4. Wicked powers assigned to waste my life in battle, die, in the name of Jesus.

5. Powers placing battles in my hand, carry your load and die, in Jesus' name.

6. O God, arise and disappoint any man working with satan to destroy my life, in the name of Jesus.

7. Environmental witchcraft, neighbourhood witchcraft caging my glory, I overcome you by the blood of Jesus, in the name of Jesus.

8. Any strange mark cursing my destiny, I tear you apart, in the name of Jesus.

PRAYER BATTLE (2)

9. Anyone lighting up an evil candle for my sake, receive the stones of fire, in the name of Jesus.

10. Every battle of 'nobody will help you', assigned against me, die, in Jesus' name.

11. Powers programming evil into my tongue, run mad and die, in Jesus' name.

12. Every satanic decree passed against my name, backfire, in the name of Jesus.

13. Every power sitting on me, receive the arrows of death, in the name of Jesus.

14. My finance, disobey the decree of darkness, in the name of Jesus.

15. Destructions, fall upon all powers giving me bad dreams, in the name of Jesus.

16. Every power raging to make me poor, die by fire, in the name of Jesus.

17. Powers giving me names that God did not give me, be silenced and die, in the name of Jesus.

18. Powers drawing strength against me, O Lord, disgrace them, in Jesus' name.

19. O God, arise and withdraw the weapons of my enemies, in the name of Jesus.

20. Arrows that will make people shake their heads in pity for me, go back to your senders, in the name of Jesus.

21. Wicked powers pouring my blessings away like water, be wasted, in the name of Jesus.

SECTION 7 - O GOD ARISE AND SILENCE MY SILENCER

Scripture Reading: Psalms 2

Confession: Psalms 31:17 Let me not be ashamed, O LORD; for I have called upon thee: let the wicked be ashamed, and let them be silent in the grave.

Day 1(08-10-21) - *The Bible in 70 Days (Day 61 - John 13:31 - Acts 1:1 - 6:3)*

Devotional Songs (Pages 4-10)

Praise and Worship

Prayers of Praise and Thanksgiving (Page 13)

1. Wicked workers of the wicked elders assigned to kill my joy, thunder of God, strike them to death, in the name of Jesus.

2. Powers waiting for my next level to make me cry, consuming fire of God, destroy them, in the name of Jesus.

3. Every agenda of the enemy to mock me, O God, delete it, in the name of Jesus.

4. Powers keeping me in the level where there is no glory, leave my life and die, in the name of a Jesus.

5. Battles celebrating that they have won over me, you are liars, be terminated, in the name of Jesus.

6. Anyone sending information on me to witches and wizards, run mad and die, in the name of Jesus.

7. Serpent of darkness rejoicing for harming me, carry your load, in Jesus' name.

8. Weapons of darkness making me to cry, be consumed by fire, in Jesus' name.

9. Powers commanding my destiny not to rise, run mad and die, in Jesus' name.

10. Dark powers of my father's house assigned to waste my glory, O Lord, tear them apart, in the name of Jesus.

11. Lion of the wicked pushing me away from my celebrations, sword of destruction, destroy it, in the name of Jesus.

12. Whatever is sustaining my enemy against me, be terminated, in Jesus' name.

13. Wicked elders committing themselves to turn my glory to disgrace, run mad, in the name of Jesus.

14. O God, arise and rebuke my strange enemies in Your anger, in Jesus' name.

15. Every cry of darkness against me, O God, silence it, in the name of Jesus.

16. Powers assigned to celebrate my nakedness, I bury you now, in Jesus' name.

17. Lion of the tribe of Judah, arise, destroy all my testimony-killers, in the name of Jesus.

18. Powers assigned to make me spend my money on battles, die, in Jesus' name.

19. Powers submitting my breakthroughs to shrines, die, in the name of Jesus.

20. Dark power shedding blood to gain control over my life, be disappointed by fire, in the name of Jesus.

21. Thunder of God, arise, swallow my strange pursuers, in the name of Jesus.

22. Powers nominating me for unending battles, die, in the name of Jesus.

23. Angry voices assigned to silence my testimony, I silence you by fire, in the name of Jesus.

24. Every disgrace waiting to replace my favour, expire, in the name of Jesus.

25. Powers that want to shorten my life with strange problems, die a woeful death, in the name of Jesus.

26. Any good thing dying in my life, wake up by fire, in the name of Jesus.

27. Powers choosing the date that I will cry, cry to death, in the name of Jesus.

28. Midnight oppression opposing my midday miracles, fall, in the name of Jesus.

Day 2 (09-10-21) - *The Bible in 70 Days (Day 62-Acts 6:4 - 17:25)*

Devotional Songs (Pages 4-10)

Praise and Worship

Prayers of Praise and Thanksgiving (Page 13)

29. Voice of disgrace hidden in my destiny, come out and catch fire, in the name of Jesus.

30. Dark battles assigned to destroy my name with shame, die, in Jesus' name.

31. Powers assigned to reduce my speed, die, in the name of Jesus.

32. O God, arise and let Your rod strike against my enemies, in the name of Jesus.

33. Powers that have vowed that I will never experience the glory of God, O Rock of Ages, grind them to powder, in the name of Jesus.

34. Anyone feeding a strange serpent against me, be consumed by your serpent,

in the name of Jesus.

35. Dark shadows flying around my life, expire by fire, in the name of Jesus.

36. Powers locking me down with chains of disappointment while my mates are moving forward, carry your load and die, in the name of Jesus.

37. Power assigned to steal my glory, lose your power and die, in Jesus' name.

38. Powers using the horns of darkness to afflict me, Lord, let their horns swallow them, in the name of Jesus.

39. Problems assigned to disgrace me before my enemies, scatter by fire, in the name of Jesus.

40. Dark power using my name and my picture to fight against me, run mad and die, in the name of Jesus.

41. Stubborn problems without solution, assigned to make life difficult for me, die, in the name of Jesus.

42. Stubborn giants parading freely in the garden of my life, be paralysed, in the name of Jesus.

43. Every power that says my prayer will always be in vain, you are a liar, die, in the name of Jesus.

44. My name, bring fear and terror upon my enemies, in the name of Jesus.

45. Every evil bird dispatched by wicked elders against my destiny, fall down and die, in the name of Jesus.

46. Every bird assigned to wipe away good things from my destiny, receive the stone of death, in the name of Jesus.

47. Spirit of the dead seeking for vengeance upon my life, blood of Jesus, destroy it, in the name of Jesus.

48. Powers of the sea dragging my destiny to the sea, release me and die, in the name of Jesus.

49. Angels of war, pursue those holding what belongs to me, in the name of Jesus.

50. Power using my glory against me, die, in the name of Jesus.

51. Battles of the wicked wasting my blessings, die, in the name of Jesus.

52. Lion of the tribe of Judah, arise, kill the lion of the wicked consuming my breakthrough, in the name of Jesus.

53. O God, silence every demonic cry assigned to shut up my laughter, in the name of Jesus.

54. Powers saying until I bow they will not let me go, O Lord, tear them to pieces, in the name of Jesus.

55. Powers sending violent battles to me, carry your load and die, in Jesus' name.

56. Every enemy planning to come into my life to destroy me, O God, arise and consume him, in the name of Jesus.

Day 3(10-10-21) - *The Bible in 70 Days (Day 63 - Acts 17:26 - Rom 1:1 - 3:1)*
Devotional Songs (Pages 4-10)
Praise and Worship
Prayers of Praise and Thanksgiving (Page 13)

57. The next enemy that will come to attack me, be consumed by fire, in the name of Jesus.

58. Any witch doctor working on my name, be frustrated by the blood of Jesus, in the name of Jesus.

59. O Lord, if I am my own enemy, arise and help me today, in the name of Jesus.

60. Powers planting evil marks in my life to kill me, die, in the name of Jesus.

61. Powers holding my vehicle of destiny to ransom, run mad and die, in the name of Jesus.

62. Power attacking me harder as I pray harder, fire of God, consume it, in the name of Jesus.

63. Acidic poverty assigned against my destiny, die, in the name of Jesus.

64. Powers bewitching my name for evil, die, in the name of Jesus.

65. Powers burning evil candles because of my glory, catch fire with your candle, in the name of Jesus.

66. Any strange power shedding blood because of me, be exposed and be disgraced, in the name of Jesus.

67. Lord, let the garments of my enemies begin to smell of hatred, in Jesus' name.

68. O God, arise and release strange fear upon my enemies to release what they have stolen from me, in the name of Jesus.

69. The sword that my enemies put their trust in shall kill them suddenly, in the

name of Jesus.

70. Lord, let death feed on the wicked elders cursing me, in the name of Jesus.

71. Arrows of great loss sent against me to make me cry, go back to your senders, in the name of Jesus.

72. Arrows assigned to make me make mistakes that cannot be corrected, backfire, in the name of Jesus.

73. Divine sword, fish out the strangers in charge of my case and kill them, in the name of Jesus.

74. Powers preparing to start all over again in my life, you shall not succeed, die suddenly, in the name of Jesus.

75. Powers that want me to help my enemies to destroy me, thunder of God, kill them, in the name of Jesus.

76. Holy Ghost, unmask every demonic agent hiding behind a mask to trouble my case, in the name of Jesus.

77. My Father, let every evil power plucking the fruit of my destiny release it and die, in the name of Jesus.

78. My days of battle, my days of sorrow, my days of affliction, your time is up, die, in the name of Jesus.

79. Powers that want to assassinate my potential, die, in the name of Jesus.

80. Eaters of flesh and drinkers of blood assigned to trouble my destiny, die, in the name of Jesus.

81. Every instrument of darkness used to put me into the den of stagnancy, catch fire, in the name of Jesus.

82. Wild animal and domestic animal in my dream, assigned to destroy my glory, I command you to die, in the name of Jesus.

83. Fire that will empower me to destroy all animals that appear in my dream, fall upon me now, in the name of Jesus.

84. Holy Ghost, blind every witchcraft bird eyeing my blessings, in Jesus' name.

Day 4 (11-10-21) - *The Bible in 70 Days (Day 64- Rom 3:2 - 1Cor 1:1 - 4:3)*

Devotional Songs (Pages 4-10)

Praise and Worship

Prayers of Praise and Thanksgiving (Page 13)

85. Every evil word uttered against me by the tongue of death, be cancelled by the blood of Jesus, in the name of Jesus.

86. I break any demonic curse upon my head, in the name of Jesus.

87. Every spiritual maggot inside my destiny, fall down and die, in Jesus' name.

88. Every problem that came into my life through the blood of my parents, die, in the name of Jesus.

89. Powers struggling to swallow me, O earth, open and swallow them, in the name of Jesus.

90. Powers of darkness marking my face for destruction, O earth, swallow them, in the name of Jesus.

91. The reproach of darkness assigned to swallow me, backfire, in Jesus' name.

92. Arrows from the tongue of wicked elders fired against me, scatter by fire, in the name of Jesus.

93. Thou sword in the lips of the wicked, terminate the wicked, in Jesus' name.

94. Strong powers of my battle, collapse and catch fire, in the name of Jesus.

95. Every secret power of the wicked assigned to waste my existence, scatter by fire, in the name of Jesus.

96. O God, arise and destroy the head of the enemy that is rising against me, in the name of Jesus.

97. Lord, let the tongue of the dogs be filled with the blood of my enemies, in the name of Jesus.

98. Powers threatening me to return what I did not take from them, O Lord, beat them to death, in the name of Jesus.

99. Whatever is protecting my enemy against me, become his trap of death, in the name of Jesus.

100. Raging anger of God, arrest the darkness following me around, in the name of Jesus.

101. Garment of darkness operating in my destiny, I tear you to pieces, in the name of Jesus.

102. You the ancestral strong man standing between me and my destiny, fall down and die, in the name of Jesus.

103. Evil soul-tie connecting me to dead people, break by the blood of Jesus, in the name of Jesus.

104. Destiny delay in my life, caused by evil dreams, break by fire, in Jesus' name.

105. Perverted destiny, disappear from my life, in the name of Jesus.

106. Warrior angels of the living God, arise, contest against all evil angels assigned against me and destroy them, in the name of Jesus.

107. Warrior angels of the living God, arise and arrest all powers harassing me, in the name of Jesus.

108. Every power closing my good doors and leaving me on the rope of stagnancy, die now, in the name of Jesus.

109. All demonic dragons working against me, be buried alive now, in the name of Jesus.

110. O God of Shadrach, Meshach and Abednego, cause my Nebuchadnezzer to perish in the fire he has made for me, in the name of Jesus.

111. Battles giving birth to battles in my life, die, in the name of Jesus.

112. Every rage against my destiny by destiny haters, expire, in Jesus' name.

Day 5 (12-10-21) - *The Bible in 70 Days (Day 65 - 1Corn 4:4 - 2Corn 1:1 - 5:3)*
Devotional Songs (Pages 4-10)
Praise and Worship
Prayers of Praise and Thanksgiving (Page 13)

113. O Lord, hide me in the blood of Jesus against wicked elders, in Jesus' name.

114. Wicked celebrations arranged to swallow my destiny, turn to madness, in the name of Jesus.

115. Powers depending on wickedness against me, divine serpent from heaven, swallow them, in the name of Jesus.

116. Wicked powers gathering with satanic agents against me, thunder of God, kill them, in the name of Jesus.

PRAYER BATTLE (2)

117. Dark powers that have made evil vows against me, die, in the name of Jesus.

118. Anyone saying that he would rather die than see me prosper, die suddenly, in the name of Jesus.

119. Powers going to native doctors to stop my star from rising, run mad and die, in the name of Jesus.

120. Strange powers fully armed against my future, die, in the name of Jesus.

121. Powers going very far to see me cry, receive the arrow of death, in the name of Jesus.

122. Mouth of darkness sucking my financial life, catch fire, in the name of Jesus.

123. Powers using my story to attack me, be disgraced, in the name of Jesus.

124. Powers that say I will never climb the ladder to the top, run mad and die, in the name of Jesus.

125. Any power visiting demonic meetings with my name, collapse and die, in the name of Jesus.

126. The wicked, standing between me and my blessings, die, in Jesus' name.

127. O God, arise and destroy the joy of the enemy celebrating over me, in the name of Jesus.

128. O Lord, send bulldozer from heaven to destroy the building of darkness standing tall against me, in the name of Jesus.

129. Lord, if I am hanging around in the kind of place that will cause me my destiny, arise and disconnect me today, in the name of Jesus.

130. O God, arise and overturn every negative consequence my destiny has suffered because of my past sins, in the name of Jesus.

131. O God, arise and overturn every negative consequence my destiny has suffered because of my parental sins, in the name of Jesus.

132. Stars from heaven, arise and fight all my battles for me, in Jesus' name.

133. Lord, let the strong men surrounding me attack themselves and destroy one another unto death, in the name of Jesus.

134. I shake off the dust of Babylon and I enter into the palace of my destiny, in the name of Jesus.

135. The unbeatable Heavenly Trinity, arise and fight my battles for me, in the

name of Jesus.

136. O four winds, carry me to the place of my glory, in the name of Jesus.

137. Rage of darkness against me, devour your owners, in the name of Jesus.

138. Rivers of my glory in high places, open by fire, in the name of Jesus.

139. Sword of fire, fly through the rage of my enemies, in the name of Jesus.

140. With the finger of fire, I point to every Herod assigned to slaughter my destiny, in the name of Jesus.

Day 6 (13-10-21) - *The Bible in 70 Days (Day 66 - 2Cor 5:4 - Eph 1:1 -5:20)*

Devotional Songs (Pages 4-10)

Praise and Worship

Prayers of Praise and Thanksgiving (Page 13)

141. Every evil gate questioning and challenging my glory, I cut you asunder, in the name of Jesus.

142. Every evil gate of my father's house, dark gate of my mother's house, I am not your candidate, catch fire, in the name of Jesus.

143. Rivers of glory, wash away my reproach and shame, in the name of Jesus.

144. Rage of failure against my success, go and consume your sender, in the name of Jesus.

145. Chains of my captivity, break by fire, in the name of Jesus.

146. Light of God, arise and kill my ignorance, in the name of Jesus.

147. Rage and furnace of affliction prepared for me, consume your owner, in the name of Jesus.

148. Sword of affliction assigned against me, devour your owner, in Jesus' name.

149. Sword of sorrow and blood assigned against me, be broken to pieces, in the name of Jesus.

150. Sword of poverty and disease assigned against me, I destroy you, in the name of Jesus.

151. Sword of divine judgement, slay all wicked prophets and their wicked prophecies against me, in the name of Jesus.

152. O God, arise and sweep away every power fighting my glory, in Jesus' name.

PRAYER BATTLE (2)

153. O God, arise and command all the haters of my destiny to run mad, in the name of Jesus.

154. Every storm programmed against the ship of my destiny, be silenced, in the name of Jesus.

155. Fainting spirit assigned to wear me out at the edge of my miracles, die by fire, in the name of Jesus.

156. I command hot angelic slap against every power pulling down my hands and weakening my prayer knees, in the name of Jesus.

157. Arrows of weak hands, I am not your candidate, backfire, in Jesus' name.

158. I command all the enemies of my destiny to scatter by fire, in Jesus' name.

159. Arise, O God, deliver the stronghold assigned against my destiny into my hands, in the name of Jesus.

160. I receive the shoe of iron and the brass of battle to trample upon the strong man, in the name of Jesus.

161. My legs, hear the word of the Lord, become the legs of the possessor and possess your holy mountain by fire, in the name of Jesus.

162. My legs, hear the word of the Lord, become the legs of the possessor and pursue your pursuers, in the name of Jesus.

163. My legs, hear the word of the Lord, become the legs of fire and burn every trap set for you on your path to possess your strong city, in Jesus' name.

164. Treasures of darkness and hidden riches of the fortified city, arise by fire and decorate my life, in the name of Jesus.

165. The enemy will pay the price that will catapult me to my place of destiny, in the name of Jesus.

166. Every fortified city harbouring my breakthroughs, I command your walls to crumble by fire, in the name of Jesus.

167. Power of the Most High, catapult me by fire above my mockers, in the name of Jesus.

168. My Father, shower my destiny this year with Your rain of mercy, in the name of Jesus.

Day 7 (14-10-21) - *The Bible in 70 Days (Day 67 - Eph 5:21 - 1Tim 1:1 - 5:5)*
Devotional Songs (Pages 4-10)
Praise and Worship
Prayers of Praise and Thanksgiving (Page 13)

169. Rain of glory, fall upon my life and wash away my shame, in Jesus' name.

170. Rain of breakthrough, fall upon me and silence my mockers, in Jesus' name.

171. Rain of divine judgement, fall upon the wicked and disgrace the strong man boasting against me, in the name of Jesus.

172. Rain of vengeance, fall with fury and burning sulphur upon my enemies, in the name of Jesus.

173. O God, arise and let Your prosperous wind carry me to my throne, in the name of Jesus.

174. Every power occupying my throne of destiny, tremble and vacate my throne, in the name of Jesus.

175. Face of mockery scaring me and laughing at me, receive the stones of fire, in the name of Jesus.

176. Power of sorrow and regret playing games with my life, die, in Jesus' name.

177. Every chronic pain fashioned to waste my virtues, perish by fire, in the name of Jesus.

178. I trample upon every stone of failure thrown at me by strangers to death, in the name of Jesus.

179. Satanic spider hiding in my body to afflict me with poverty, come out and die, in the name of Jesus.

180. Every barren situation in my life, be fruitful by fire, in the name of Jesus.

181. Every evil power drawing lines to mark out my life, go blind, in Jesus' name.

182. Every stubborn affliction assigned to bury me, die, in the name of Jesus.

183. Every power using the secret of midnight to attack me, sleep and never wake up, in the name of Jesus.

184. Every power multiplying troubles for my life, be consumed by fire, in the name of Jesus.

185. Battles that are too strong for me, I hand you over to the Rock of Ages, in the

name of Jesus.

186. Power of unstoppable testimonies, fall upon my life, in the name of Jesus.

187. My Father, let Your grace terminate my disgrace, in the name of Jesus.

188. Every river of affliction in my life, I dry you to death, in the name of Jesus.

189. Power of roaring poverty assigned to bury my talents, die, in Jesus' name.

190. Anything in my life that is feeding my problems, die, in the name of Jesus.

191. Every evil power that is partly responsible for my ignorance, die, in the name of Jesus.

192. Powers using dark prayers to disturb my progress, die, in the name of Jesus.

193. Any power assigned to quench the light of my destiny, be terminated, in the name of Jesus.

194. I kill the peace of my enemies, by the power in the blood of Jesus, in the name of Jesus.

195. Any power feeding evil trees against me, I place a death notice upon you, in the name of Jesus.

196. Agents of darkness holding ancestral records against me, catch fire, in the name of Jesus.

Day 8 (15-10-21) - *The Bible in 70 Days (Day 68 - 1Tim 5:6 - Heb 1:1 - 11:40)*
Devotional Songs (Pages 4-10)
Praise and Worship
Prayers of Praise and Thanksgiving (Page 13)

197. Every evil command from any wicked mouth against me, scatter, in the name of Jesus.

198. Every ancient tree receiving sacrifices because of me, sword of God, cut it down, in the name of Jesus.

199. My virtues kept in the tree of darkness, come out and locate me now, in the name of Jesus.

200. Every tree standing against me on my success journey, sword of fire, cut it down, in the name of Jesus.

201. Breeze of wicked elders sweeping my testimonies away, catch fire, in the name of Jesus.

202. Witchcraft defecation upon my head, blood of Jesus, wash it away, in the name of Jesus.

203. Sacrifices offered to feed demons for my sake, lose your power over me, in the name of Jesus.

204. Dagon, god of the waters, any sacrifice you have received on behalf of my life, I destroy it, in the name of Jesus.

205. Strange trees hosting the meetings of wicked elders against me, receive acidic fire, in the name of Jesus.

206. Evil powers that planted themselves in my life, uncommon death, clear them out of my life, in the name of Jesus.

207. Every tree shaking the ground against my destiny, catch fire, in Jesus' name.

208. O God, release Your thunder on any evil tree of my father's house, where my glory has been sacrificed, in the name of Jesus.

209. Powers that have swallowed demons and are threatening me, thunder of God, swallow them, in the name of Jesus.

210. Birds of darkness entering into each other to form a single body to attack me, storm of fire, swallow them up, in the name of Jesus.

211. Witchcraft powers using cobwebs to sew a garment for me, run mad and die, in the name of Jesus.

212. Throne of wickedness in my father's house, catch fire, in the name of Jesus.

213. Hired wicked powers against my life, die, in the name of Jesus.

214. The battle that swallowed my father, you will not swallow me, in the name of Jesus.

215. Ancestral mark in my body, attracting demonic bird into my house, expire, in the name of Jesus.

216. Champions of my father's house, who have vowed not to see me succeed in life, die by fire, in the name of Jesus.

217. Ancestral murder tormenting the destiny of children in my lineage, die, in the name of Jesus.

218. Cobwebs of darkness tying my hands for untimely death, come out and catch fire, in the name of Jesus.

219. Powers beating their chest that I will die rather than rise, die in my place, in the name of Jesus.

220. Anyone writing my name on the body of an animal, to bury it alive so as to kill me, die with the animal, in the name of Jesus.

221. Deep sea swallowing my virtues, vomit them by fire, in the name of Jesus.

222. Book of generational failure bearing my name, catch fire, in Jesus' name.

223. Every child of darkness covering my future, run mad by fire, in Jesus' name.

224. Evil hand behind evil pregnancy in my life, be cut off, in the name of Jesus.

Day 9 (16-10-21) - *The Bible in 70 Days (Day 69 - Heb 12:1 - 2Joh 1:1 - 1:11)*
Devotional Songs (Pages 4-10)
Praise and Worship
Prayers of Praise and Thanksgiving (Page 13)

225. Evil hands responsible for the problems in my life, die, in the name of Jesus.

226. Evil assignments of the enemy for my life, be terminated, in Jesus' name.

227. I remove my name from the book of those who see good things but do not receive them, in the name of Jesus.

228. Hands of the wicked elders pushing my head down as I try to lift it up, catch fire, in the name of Jesus.

229. Anyone collecting graveyard sand against me, be disgraced, in Jesus' name.

230. Dark powers of the grave, get out of my way now, in the name of Jesus.

231. Every image of my life in the graveyard, catch fire, in the name of Jesus.

232. Coffin arrows sent against me, backfire, in the name of Jesus.

233. Enemies holding me, hold me no more, in the name of Jesus.

234. Powers assigned to cover me with the garment of battles, be consumed by fire, in the name of Jesus.

235. Celebration of the wicked elders assigned to make me cry, turn to madness, in the name of Jesus.

236. Every door that will lead to my destiny, hear the word of the Lord, open by fire, in the name of Jesus.

237. The will of the enemy shall not come to pass on my head, in Jesus' name.

238. Powers struggling to kill my life, die, in the name of Jesus.

239. Every power assigned against the divine oil on my head, die, in Jesus' name.

240. Powers pursuing my head for evil exchange, die, in the name of Jesus.

241. My Father, arise in Your fire and move my life forward, in the name of Jesus.

242. Hidden mockers playing with me to attack me unawares, O God, expose and disappoint them, in the name of Jesus.

243. Mockers using their poisonous tongues to laugh at me, O Lord, tear them to pieces, in the name of Jesus.

244. Mockers assigned to turn me to a victim of disgrace, be destroyed, in the name of Jesus.

245. Battles mocking me to make me a reproach, die, in the name of Jesus.

246. O God, arise and use my life to disgrace the mockers, in the name of Jesus.

247. My enemies shall hear my testimonies and run mad, in the name of Jesus.

248. O Lord, give me the victory that will turn my battles to testimonies, in the name of Jesus.

249. Powers setting me up to deny God so as to enslave me the more, O God, destroy them with Your anger, in the name of Jesus.

250. Powers that want good people to forget me, O God, tear them apart, in the name of Jesus.

251. Anyone rejoicing at my long-time difficulties, O Lord, use Your knife to disappoint them, in the name of Jesus.

252. O Lord, use Your hand to draw me out of the waters of trouble, in the name of Jesus.

Day 10 (17-10-21) - *The Bible in 70 Days (Day 70 - 2 Joh 1:12 - Rev 1:1-22:21)*
Devotional Songs (Pages 4-10)
Praise and Worship
Prayers of Praise and Thanksgiving (Page 13)

253. Lord, let the blood of my enemy arise and waste him, in the name of Jesus.

254. Powers standing naked to undress me, run mad and die, in Jesus' name.

255. Powers hiding and smiling at my sufferings, O Lord, expose them and let them die in disgrace, in the name of Jesus.

256. The kind of disgrace that my enemy deserves, O Lord, give it to him, in the name of Jesus.

257. O God, arise and let my enemies dance in disgrace, in the name of Jesus.

258. O Lord, do not let it be too late for me before You deliver me, in the name of Jesus.

259. Powers saying, 'congratulations' is an abomination for me, be disappointed and die, in the name of Jesus.

260. Powers saying my battles will continue until I say there is no God, O God, strike them to death, in the name of Jesus.

261. Powers assigned to make me spend my money on battles, fall down and die, in the name of Jesus.

262. My Father, my Father, my Father, no devourer is permitted to waste my life, in the name of Jesus.

263. Anything in my life that is cooperating with the spirit of the devourer to fight against me, come out and die, in the name of Jesus.

264. I decree and declare that wasters shall not waste my life; emptiers shall not empty my life; destroyers shall not destroy my life, in the name of Jesus.

265. Financial demon plaguing my destiny, come out and die, in Jesus' name.

266. Arrows of financial debt assigned against my income, die, in Jesus' name.

267. Powers trying to frustrate my life with dark prayers, O God, fail them, in the name of Jesus.

268. The wall of disgrace and poverty fashioned against me, collapse and fail, in the name of Jesus.

269. You, devourers hear the word of the Lord, vanish from my labour, in the name of Jesus.

270. Powers that have vowed to deal with anyone that wants to help me, run mad and die, in the name of Jesus.

271. Battles increasing my silent tears, die, in the name of Jesus.

272. My glory that has been kept in a cage since I was born, come out and locate me, in the name of Jesus.

273. O Lord, terrify my enemies as they are rejoicing on their evil plans against

me, in the name of Jesus.

274. O God, arise and frustrate all the struggling of my enemies against me, in the name of Jesus.

275. Powers seeking my head for evil arrows, die, in the name of Jesus.

276. Every spirit of the mortuary hanging upon me and my helpers, die, in the name of Jesus.

277. O hand of God, arise and drive out of my life, every evil hand inviting dark visitors into my life, in the name of Jesus.

278. Every evil word fighting against my destiny, go back to your sender, in the name of Jesus.

279. Thorns of darkness growing in the field of my destiny, clear away and catch fire, in the name of Jesus.

280. Begin to thank God for answers to all your prayers as this year's seventy days prayer and fasting programme comes to an end.

SECTION CONFESSIONS

No counsel of the wicked shall stand against me, in the name of Jesus. Unto me, shall God do exceedingly abundantly above all that I ask, seek, desire and think, according to the power that He had made to work in me, in the name of Jesus. As it is written, I shall be a crown of glory in the hand of God, a royal diadem in the hand of my Maker. I begin to shine like a shining light. The light of God is in me. The word of God has made me a brazen wall, a fortified city, an iron pillar. My presence terrifies the enemy. He trembles, feels much pain and travails at the sound of my voice which the Lord has empowered. For it is written, wherever the voice of the king is, there is authority. My appearance is as the appearance of a horse. So, I leap and I run like mighty men. When I fall upon the sword, it cannot hurt me, in the name of Jesus.

God has equipped me and made me a danger and terror to all my enemies, in the name of Jesus. The Lord is my light and my salvation, whom shall I fear? The Lord is the strength of my life; of whom shall I be afraid? When the wicked, even mine enemies and foes, come upon me to eat up my flesh, they stumble and fall, in the name of Jesus. I pursue my enemies; I overtake and destroy them, in Jesus' name. The Lord has lifted me and I am seated with Him in heavenly places in Christ Jesus, far above principalities, powers and dominion, and the Lord has put all things under my feet, and I use my feet to bruise and destroy all my enemies, even satan, in the name of Jesus. In Jesus' name, anywhere the soles of my feet shall tread upon, the Lord has given it unto me.

SECTION VIGIL

(To be done at night between the hours of 12 midnight and 2 am)

HYMN FOR THE VIGIL (Pages 10-11)

1. O God, draw out Your sword against evil powers preparing me for reproach, in the name of Jesus.

2. Any reproach in my life, as a result of the mistakes of my parents die, in Jesus' name.

3. Powers feeding on my testimonies and commanding me to dance in reproach, die, in the name of Jesus.

4. O Lord, let those who hate me see Your great wonders in me, in Jesus' name.

5. Those who are close to me and want to see me suffering, O Lord, lock them up in disgrace forever, in the name of Jesus.

6. Weeping shall not replace laughter in my life, in the name of Jesus.

7. Weeping shall replace the laughter of the wicked, in the name of Jesus.

8. Powers that do not want me to know the origin of my problems, run mad and die, in the name of Jesus.

9. Powers that want me to worship God in suffering, die, in the name of Jesus.

10. Battles that have vowed to kill me at the end, die, in the name of Jesus.

11. Those who envy me and wish me untimely death, die suddenly, in Jesus' name.

12. Every curse in my family that is making me suffer, break by fire, in the name of Jesus.

13. O Lord, silence every idol cursing me and my family day and night, in the name of Jesus.

14. Family battles assigned to bury my head, release my head and die, in the name of Jesus.

15. Dangerous power from my foundation, holding the keys of my destiny, release them and die, in the name of Jesus.

16. O Lord, give me the glory that will make me important among my family and those who hate, in the name of Jesus.

17. O Lord, let my glory kill the glory of the enemy, in the name of Jesus.

18. My glory and the lifter of my head, arise and lift me, in the name of Jesus.

19. Garment of financial barrenness, catch fire, in the name of Jesus.

20. Powers controlling my journey to stop me from prospering, die, in the name of Jesus.

21. Covenant of the blood assigned against me, break, in the name of Jesus.